NAVEEN PATNAIK

The Iconic CM of India

RAZIQUE HOSAIN SHAIKH

INDIA · SINGAPORE · MALAYSIA

ISBN

Hardcase 979-8-89322-831-1
Paperback 979-8-89322-652-2

Dedicated To

My Loving parents
Shaikh Gollam Rabani
Asira Khatun

Courtesy: Biswa Pratap Singh

***Tum Mahaktey Raho Fizaon main Tarrannum-E-Zamhuriat Ban Kar
Lutatey Raho Apni Shaadgi Watan Pe Paikar-E-Sachayee Ban Kar…***

– Razique Hosain Shaikh

Contents

Author's Note 9

Prologue 17

1 – A Tribute to the Legend..................21

2 – How and When Naveen Enter into Politics…? 29

3 – Opponents Said, Naveen Babu Zindabaad..................37

4 – 5T-Initiative 55

5 – Heart Winning Welfare Schemes..................67

6 – Odisha – Naveen, Naveen – Odisha, A Role Model 133

7 – Odisha Millets Mission 149

8 – 2024 – A Milestone to Achieve..................157

Acknowledgement 169

Precious Memories 171

Author's Note

This is my 5th book that I'm about to start writing. I have written two books related to cooking. Because cooking is my profession and I'm engaged in this field since more than two decades. So I did not face any special difficulties in writing cooking books. And the other two books are fictional novels about rural love stories. Writing stories has been my passion since childhood. So, I didn't have to face much trouble or any extra labor to write novels.

Actually, I realized that it is easier to write non-fiction than fiction. After all, in non-fiction, you are dealing with a story that already exists, you don't have to invent the twists and turns. With this thought, I started writing this non-fictional unauthorized biography of our beloved and popular leader. With the hope that I can write this book very easily, I started writing very comfortably but as my writing progressed, my anxiety increased gradually. Along with that my accountability and responsibility increased to a great extent. Perhaps, that's the reason why I had to work harder to write this book as compared to my earlier four books.

Still I could not stop myself from writing this biography. Because that personality is so generous that of course his fans and well-wishers love him, admire him but the best part is that his political opponents are also bound to admire and praise him. Even his opponents do not hold back in praising.

I proudly do not hesitate in acknowledging that, what a big fan I am of Mr. Naveen Patnaik, The Hon'ble Chief Minister of Odisha!

Firstly, I would like to mention those two incidents which forced me to write this book. An incident after which I could not stop myself from writing this biography. Although I had no experience at all in biography writing. I had to face a lot of trouble and hard work, still I was unable to stop my pen from writing this biography.

One of those incidents caused immense pain, embarrassed me and broke my heart but the later lifted my spirits and made me feel so proud.

Flash back to the past two decades…

Actually, this matter is of 2004-05. I was in Dubai. That was the beginning of my career so I was doing some small job there in Dubai. That day was my weekly off so I went to a super market named LULU for some casual shopping. LULU is a very famous supermarket in the gulf countries. Fortunately, the owner was an Indian from the state Kerala. And most of the people who worked in this supermarket belong to Kerala.

After picking up my goods I took my shopping cart and headed towards the cash counter. When I reached at the cash counter, there were two people ahead of me and I was the third one waiting in queue.

As I told most of the employees there were from Kerala so the cashier was also from Kerala. And the best part was that the two customers standing ahead of me with their cart were also from India. One was from Mumbai and the other from Bihar. And as we know, whenever we Indians meet each other abroad, whether we know the person or not, we start our casual discussion with each other.

The same thing happened with all four of us and within a few moments we started interacting with each other. Although the cashier was continuously punching goods in scanner for billing still he was involved in our discussion with his broken Hindi. Meanwhile, all of us asked each other a very common question. Which is mandatory question of every discussion in foreign countries for us. And that is, each one of us were from which state?

Of the two people standing in front of me, one said he was from Mumbai and the other person was from Bihar. And I said, "I am from Odisha". Actually, now the turn was of the cashier to tell us which state of India he is from but instead of telling the name of his home state. Maybe he knows, that there is no need to tell that he was from Kerala. So maybe that's why his question jumped two person standing ahead of me and is pointed at me from the cash counter and asked,

Where is Odisha...???

Is it in Kolkata, West Bengal...???

I Razique Hosain Shaikh from Odisha, India, who was involved in that very casual discussion of few Indian in a foreign Country, United Arab Emirate's one state known as Dubai.

Maybe that was a very small question for that cashier but, but that question shook my existence! I was stunned. I certainly felt sad and embarrassed, but along with it I also felt regretful that how is this possible? A citizen living in India does not know where Odisha is? Odisha is not a district or a village's name. Odisha, the 8th largest state of India with an area of 155,707 sq.km. Odisha, the 11th largest state of India by population with over 47.92 million (approx.) people. Odisha, the state with 30 districts.

There are so many countries in the world which are smaller than a district of my state.

Odisha, Such a great state with a glorious history of thousands of years. Land of so many brave great heroes. Land of culture, land of art, land of religion.

How can an Indian can say that, where is Odisha?

Why did I had to face such a challenging and sad question?

Is our state really that backward? That people of our own country don't know where it is?

Have we really not done any such work which would bring recognition to our state in our own country?

Who is responsible for this?

Many such bitter questions were piercing my heart and mind!

With immense sadness and lots of such raised questions in my mind, I came back to my room from the shopping mall. That cashier's question was giving me a strange pain in my heart. That in what state I am living in? Forget about the people of other country, people of our own country don't know where Odisha is?

It was very insulting and embarrassing incident that day for me. It felt as if someone had rubbed smashed green chilies into my body.

Anyway, what can I do now other than digesting that pain and embarrassment silently? Gradually this thing got blurred in my mind and I got busy in my routine life. Everything got normal in life. Same job, family, money, vacations etc. Everything was going on so normal and peacefully.

Yes of course, two big changes came in my life. Firstly, I shifted from Dubai to Sultanate of Oman. And secondly, my childhood dream which was buried somewhere, after shifting to Oman got alive again. Yes, 'writing', after coming to Oman I wrote many books, novels, cooking books etc.

In between decades passed and after two decades the same incident happened again which indeed reminded me the painful tragedy of

Dubai but it also gave me a way to forget that sorrow. And gave me a great opportunity to be happy and feel proud.

Actually, what happened is that, the sad incident which took place in a supermarket two decades ago happened again.

Everything looked so cinematic!

I was working in Muscat, the capital of Sultanate of Oman with MHD Group. There is a very big and well-known supermarket named *Sultan Center*. And I had bought a multipurpose oven and griller from that super market for my company. But within a few days we found some technical fault in that machine. So I reached to the supermarket along with the defective machine and warranty papers to exchange that piece.

When I reached at the customer service counter, The Omani girl in there in the counter told me in Arabic that *"hadhih mas'alat kabirat bayed alshay, lidhalik sayatayeayan ealayk altahaduth 'iilaa rayiys fareina"* (this is a little big matter, so for this you will have to talk to our branch head).

"Ok, so who is your branch head and where can I find him?" I asked her in my half broken Arabic talking knowledge.

"Alsayid Michael Joseph hu rayiys fareina. Mae hadhih al'waraqat yurjaa aldhahab 'iilaa maktabih waltahaduth maeahu" (Mr. Michael Joseph is our branch head. Along with this papers you please go to his office and talk to him). That Omani Girl said.

"Shkraan jzylaan" (thank you so much) I will talk to him". I said to the Arabic girl and turned back to go to the branch manager's office.

"eafwan ya sayidi, 'hu alsayidu Michael, mudir fareina. Yumkinuk altahaduth maeah" (Excuse me sir, he is Mr. Michael our branch manager. You can talk to him). A man more than six feet height, healthy, dark walking towards us, near the customer service counter. Pointing towards the man, the girl said to me.

"*sayidi, yurid tabdil alfurn bisabab baedal mashakil al tiqniaal faniyat fi alfurn*". (Sir, he wants to exchange the oven due to some technical issues in it). The girl said to the branch manager while introducing him to me at the same time.

"Hello sir, no problem. Please show me the warranty paper. We will exchange that for you." The manager said to me.

"Hello Mr. Michael, here are the papers, please check." I said.

"Are you Indian?" Mr. Michael ask me.

"Yes, I am Indian." I said.

"I think you are also from India." I asked him.

"Yes, I am too from India, Goa." Mr. Michael said.

"I am from Odisha." I said in a little low voice. Because suddenly I remembered my old wound of Dubai. I just felt like maybe Mr. Michael wouldn't know where Odisha is. So I said out of shy.

But I remained silent and shocked after seeing Mr. Michael's answer and reaction of his face.

"Oh My God, you are from Odisha. I am really glad to meet you. What a state, what a Chief minister, what a personality, I am a big fan of your Chief Minister Mr. Naveen Patnaik. I really feel proud that we have leader like him in our country. I have very deep interest in our country's politics and my biggest wish is to see Mr. Patnaik as our Prime Minister."

"Please let's go to my cabin Mr. Hosain and don't worry about your oven, I will exchange that for you and deliver. I will not let you go so easily, hahaha…!"

Forcing me Mr. Michael took me to his cabin. I don't understand what he thinks of me but he kept talking about my state Odisha and our CM Mr. Naveen Patnaik. Mr. Michael told me such things about my state and our Chief Minister which I myself did not know. He kept praising my state's Chief Minister and kept counting his every work for hours.

I was feeling a bit embarrassed as he was describing me such details about my own state which I did not know myself. But at the same time there was a strange happiness I felt in my heart. I was feeling very proud of my state and our Hon'ble Chief Minister Naveen Patnaik. There was no limit of my happiness that day.

Someone was praising my state and my state's Chief Minister so much in a foreign land, hearing that my chest swelled with pride.

During our conversation Mr. Michael Joseph came to know that I am a writer then he forcefully requested me to write the biography of our beloved Chief Minister Naveen Patnaik.

And of course there was no scope to refuse or any chance to say no to him after hearing such golden words about our own great leader!

Actually, the truth is that I myself became so emotional after talking to him that I myself was deeply interested for such attempt. Something similar was going on in my mind that I should write about our CM to convey respect to such a great leader, to a living legend.

Mr. Michael Joseph left me that day with a promise that I would start writing a biography of our beloved CM Mr. Naveen Patnaik soon and I will gift the first copy of the book to him.

After that day I started my preparation. Tried a lot to know about our hero, our Iconic Chief Minister.

My years of hard work paid off and as a result this beautiful book is in your hand which you are reading now. I hope that you will love my work and appreciate my hard work.

For me that day will not be less than a fare and festival when I will get an opportunity to gift this extremely beautiful book in the hand of our great leader, Hon'ble Chief Minister Mr. Naveen Patnaik.

Thank you!

Prologue

Odisha proclaims a glorious historical and cultural lineage spanning 2000 years or more. Odisha the 11th largest populated state of India with a total estimated population as per the Aadhaar statistics in 2022/2023 45.43 million approximately. The 8th largest state by area with 155,707 SQ KM in the country.

From Asoka to Narasimha Deva and Mukunda Deva Harichandana to Mughal rule, Marathas and British rule. Several great empires and dynasties have ruled over the state and have contributed greatly to the history, culture and development of Odisha.

In 1885, Indian National Congress was founded. In 1920, it adopted reorganization of provinces according to linguistic basis as one of its agendas. This inspired many leaders in Odisha to form an Odisha congress committee and demand a separate province for the Odia speaking population.

And finally on 1st April 1936 Odisha (Formerly known Orissa) became a separate province. That's why 1st April is being celebrated as Utkal divas (Foundation day) of Odisha after a long struggle. After the foundation, the province has been controlled by the king of Paralakhemundi, Maharaja Krishna Chandra Gajapati Narayana Deo. He ruled the province just until July 1937.

Thereafter the all India congress party leader Bishwanath Das took charge for two more years and then again Maharaja Krishna Chandra Gajapati Narayana Deo took the control. But again in few years only he finally handed over to Dr. Harekrushna Mahatab in the year 1946.

After India got its freedom and constitution was enacted, the state started working in the principals of democracy. Until the first election Dr. Harekrushna Mahatab continued to be the chief minister of Odisha and then Mr. Nabakrushna Choudhury in 1950 was elected as the Chief Minister.

Since then till today Odisha has witnessed many elections, many great leaders have come and gone. From Dr. Harekrushna Mahatab to Naveen Patnaik, many great leaders from different political party became chief minister of this state. Since 1946, Odisha has seen 14 chief ministers and has been under president's rule for six times over a short period of time. Everyone served this state in their own way by occupying the seat of chief minister. Everyone tried to develop Odisha on their own lines while being the chief minister.

As we can remember Nandini Satpathy (the only female chief minister of Odisha) served Odisha for two terms (from 1972 to 1976 and from 1980 to 1985). During her tenure as chief minister she implemented various development and welfare measure in Odisha. Nandini Satpathy focused on improving the education system, rural development, healthcare infrastructure in the state. She actively promoted women empowerment and worked toward the upliftment of marginalized communities.

Similarly, other chief minister has also done a lot towards the development of Odisha.

But if we remember Biju Patnaik then his list is very long and glorious. Either it maybe in politics, industrial development or personal achievements. We Odias not only remember him as a successful chief minister of Odisha but his bravery and valor has also been quite golden and splendid. Which cannot be summed up in few lines. Indeed, we will discuss some more stories of his bravery further. Because without discussing and knowing about Biju Babu neither Naveen Babu nor BJD is incomplete.

And as far as Mr. Naveen Patnaik is concerned as chief minister of Odisha. He has gone four steps ahead of even his father, of course. The dream that Biju Babu had seen about a successful and modern Odisha. Naveen Babu definitely seems determined to fulfill the dream. He is greatly committed to fulfilling those dreams. Mr. Naveen Patnaik is walking on the same footsteps as his father. His development and administrative records are exemplary and splendid.

As this book is all about Mr. Naveen Patnaik's biography. Let's begin quickly. Solet's discuss the political journey of Naveen Babu. From 1997 Aska constituency's by-election to 2019 assembly and Lok Sabha election. From becoming a member of parliament (MP) to the longest serving chief minister of Odisha's political history and second longest serving chief minister in India till date.

We will try to find out that how he running the state for so long.

In such a cut-throat political era he is ruling in hearts of 4.5 crores of Odia since more than two decades.

What else does Mr. Naveen Patnaik have, apart from his powerful surname that since more than twenty years the people of Odisha trusted him blindly and wanted to see him as their chief minister again and again?

Secondly we will also try to know that why Naveen Babu had to step into politics leaving Delhi's glittering party life?

The thing that Mr. Naveen Patnaik was never interested in; then suddenly why did he have to join it after the age of 50?

Mr. Naveen Patnaik, who stayed away from politics for 50-52 years of his life. Suddenly what was that compulsion and under what circumstances he had to come into politics?

And when he entered politics, he never looked back!

He won every election one after the other and reached a new height every time. Mr. Naveen Patnaik kept setting a new ample of success every time. And with great strength, he has made a place for himself in the heart of the people of Odisha.

Which has become almost impossible to break the record…!

1 – A Tribute to the Legend

Precious glimpses of Naveen Patnaik's Mother Gyan Patnaik and his legendary father Mr. Biju Patnaik.

Courtesy: SAMBAD, Published on: Mar 3, 2016

Bijayananda Patnaik (Biju Patnaik) son of Lakshminarayana Patnaik and Ashalata Patnaik, a restless son and a legendary hero of Odisha. A true statesman, a philanthropist. He was born in Cuttack, Odisha on march 5th 1916 at his ancestral home "Anand Bhavan" Tulasipur in Cuttack. Biju Patnaik's parents belonged to Bhanjanagar in Gunjam. He had inherited this all extraordinary persona from his father, because his father Lakshminarayana Patnaik too was a great nationalist and a prominent leader of the Odia movement. He has close link with Utkal Gourav Madhusudan Das and Utkalamani Gopabandhu Das (the two architects of modern Odisha).

As I have mentioned earlier that neither we can talk about Naveen Babu nor the existence of BJD without discussing about the great intellectual legislature, the tallest leader of post-independent Odisha. The Biju Janata Dal is incomplete without the illustrious son of India. Not only the party BJD has been named after Biju Babu, but his secular views and ideology are also the main pillar of the party.

So that's why we will move forward while paying tribute to the hero of Kalinga-the Kharvela of Kalinga-Bijayananda Patnaik-Biju Patnaik-Bhumi Putra-Satabdhi Purush. Actually he had so many names but he was very well recognized as *"Biju Babu"*. Everyone in Odisha fondly called him Biju Babu. Biju Babu, Brave son of Utkal, lifelong public representative, popular politician of Odisha, former Chief Minister and the gentle artisans of modern Odisha, *"Biju Babu"*.

Not only in Odisha, he was uncontestant persona of Indian National politics. Odisha was his laboratory. Biju Babu was the inter-caste acquaintances of Odisha. Early school life in Cuttack's Mission School and Ravenshaw collegiate school. Beginning of higher education in Ravenshaw college.

In 1934 Biju Babu left Ravenshaw collage after completing his intermediate of science. Biju Babu was fascinated by aeroplane from his childhood. From his very early days of school he was determined to be a pilot. Because of his strong determination to become a pilot, Biju Babu dropped his B.Sc. degree to start training as a pilot at the Aeronautic Training Institute of India, Delhi flying club.

In 1936 after completing his aeronautics engineering, he started his career with Indian National Airways. Subsequently Biju Babu became a pilot of Indian Air Force.

After two years, in 1938 Biju Babu got married to Gyan Devi. Though Gyan Patnaik is remembered as the wife of Biju Patnaik but on her own she was one of the greatest woman of India during the 1930s.

Gyan Patnaik was not only the great mother of three siblings Prem Patnaik, Geeta Patnaik and Naveen Patnaik but also she was among the first few women commercial pilots of India. She was very courageous, inspirational, daring and down to earth woman.

The biggest proof of her bravery is that she was accompanied Biju Babu stubbornly when he went on that dangerous mission to Indonesia. She co-piloted her brave husband in his historic rescue operation. Tribute to the great mother.

Mr. Biju Patnaik was a bravest, daring hearted and a visionary person. While studying ISc in Ravenshaw college, Cuttack along with two of his friends, he left for Peshawar on bicycle. Which was a burning example of his bravery.

He was expert pilot, a true freedom fighter a patriot, a successful industrialist and a true leader. Especially his dream was to make Odisha a developed and superior state of the country. Inspite of being the Chief Minister for two times he continued his effort till his last breath.

Paradeep port is one of his dream's example. For which he had to advocated a lot to the central government. Wherever Odisha has reached today in the field of development, Biju Babu's hidden dream is locating inside.

Not only Paradeep port, NALCO, MIG Factory, transmission of Rourkela Ispat Factory, OUAT Regional Research Laboratory, Sainik School, thermal power plant, Engineering college at Rourkela etc. The vocational education center in the state is the developed wings of Biju Babu's dreams in the field of research and industrial expansion.

Along with this conferring Kalinga Award with the help of UNESCO is measured as a prestigious award by the international scientific community. In the year 1945 he created an industrialization atmosphere in Odisha by establishing Odisha Textile Mill, OTM. Biju Babu developed his industrial business back to back after establishing Kalinga Airlines and Kalinga Tubes. But in the future, after entering into full phase politics, he gradually moved out of his business.

In true sense Biju Babu was the eagle in a storm. A person who leaves the old path and creates the new ones. Despite being a pilot of Royal Airforce in the British government, at that time he could not hide the consciousness for independent India within himself.

During the quit India movement without British Government's knowledge, he was transporting secretly the front rows freedom fighter leaders, Jay Prakash Narayana, Ram Manohar Lohiya and Aruna Asha Parekh to different places by his plane.

Similarly, inspired by the ideology of Subhas Chandra Boss, Biju Babu used to drop flyers of Azaad Hind Fouz from sky in place to place while he was flying his plane. After knowing all these activities, not only he had to lose his job but also British Government jailed him. Biju Babu was a true national leader. Whenever there has been a call for the independence and integrity of the country, at that time Biju Babu was searched.

In 1947, Pakistan Army's nefarious attempt to capture Kashmir had stirred India. On the advice of Prime Minister Nehru, he took his plane and flew directly towards Srinagar. Despite of the objections of many people, he landed his plane in Srinagar valley, this not only boosted the moral of the Indian Air Force but also played an important role in pushing back the enemies.

When the Netherlands launched a massive invasion to capture Indonesia. At that time under the leadership of president Dr Sukarno, Indonesians were struggling for freedom from the Dutch.

India was supporting Indonesia's freedom struggle. Dr. Sukarno instructed the Prime Minister Dr Sjahrir and vice president Dr Hatta to discuss with the Indian leadership the issue of inter-racial aid. But the Dutch army was controlling the Indonesian land, sea and air routes. To solve this problem Dr Sukarno requested to the Indian Prime Minister Pandit Jawaharlal Nehru.

Then Pandit Nehru requested to his most trusted Biju Babu. Because of Pandit Nehru's request, Biju Babu took his Dakota plane and left towards Indonesia. Leaving her newborn baby boy with the nanny, Biju's wife Gyan Patnaik was adamant in going with him as his Co-Pilot. Biju couple crossed the seven seas and flew towards Indonesia in their Dakota plane.

Every moment of life was threatening. Even when the plane ran out of petrol, he landed his Dakota at a temporary air base in Indonesia and used the leftover petrol lying in japans military dump during the time of world war. Despite of disaster situation everywhere he got success in two days. Finally, he flew back to Delhi via Singapore with the house arrested Indonesian Prime Minister Dr Sjahrir and vice president Dr Hatta.

While he was flying back the Dutch Air Force rained a lot of bullets and ammunition over Biju Babu's Dakota. But defeating their continues attack, skilled pilot Biju Babu managed to land them safely at Delhi. After that, public opinion started against Dutch all over the world. And then Indonesia got freedom from the Dutch.

After getting freedom from Dutch, the Indonesian President Dr Sukarno honored Biju Babu massively. Biju Babu was given honorary citizenship in Indonesia and awarded the *"Bhumi Putra"* (the highest Indonesian award, rarely granted to a foreigner).

Not only this, the Indonesian Government gifted him lands, property, palace worth of crores but Biju Babu refused to accept. But Biju Babu's name and his bravery stories are written in golden words in the history of Indonesia's independence struggle.

Mr. Biju Patnaik was not only known as an unparalleled leader in Indian level, he was a live example of immense courage and bravery, whose influence had reached beyond India's border to the other countries of world. After crossing thousands of kilometers during the second world war, together with the Russian army, he fought against Hitler's army and gave proof of his bravery.

For which he was later honored by the Russian government also. Biju was a symbol of enthusiasm among Odia people. In one line he was a matchless politician, along with a freedom fighter he was a splendid pilot. Because of this he has left golden impressions in country and outside the country as well.

Biju Babu had proven himself as a skilled pilot just within three years of his piloting education. After this he joined Royal Indian Air Force. After joining Royal Indian Air Force Biju Babu had become the first choice number one pilot of highest ranking officers of Governor General posts in the British Government.

After this second world war was started a few years later. The whole world was divided into two parts in the second world war. Japan, Germany, Italy was on one side and on the other side were the British, America and Russia.

There was a fierce fight between the two sides. At that time, despite of India's independence movement reached its peak, India supported the British. Biju Babu was at the forefront from India's side in this war.

Biju Babu got Pandit Nehru's call while India was supporting England and its allies' countries in the second world. Following Nehru's request, Biju reached Russia and started fighting against the Nazi army.

The Nazi army was very powerful at the beginning of second world war. Soviet Russia was disintegrated due to the rapid attack of Nazi's head

Hitler. At that time, Biju Babu had reached there with his plane. There, amazing audacious tactics were shown in the battle against Hitler's army in the battlefields like Moscow and chunking and he became a hero for Russia.

Russian had not forgotten the bravery shown by Biju Babu during the second world war. That's why the Russian government honored to this brave man by the prestigious award of Russia. He was the first Odia to be honored with such an international honor. During the second world war Biju Babu's role was not limited to this.

At that time few British families were held captive by Japan. Biju had rescued them all very wisely from there. After rescuing them, they were all safely transported near the British authority in Delhi. For this he was later honored by the British Government also.

These were some precious achievements and golden memories of Biju Babu's life. Well, it is not possible to write them completely. Just a little effort of mine to touch the few milestones of the brave man.

Whether Biju Babu remains in power or not. He had an unwavering influence in the national politics. At one time he was the king maker of Indian politics. No matter how much he flew in the national and international sky but his heart was pure and true Odia.

Biju was not only a brave man, a skilled pilot or a great leader but he was an emotional and soft hearted person. His distinct contact with the common people, national sentiments and his wonderful heart had taken him far above the politics and power.

This pilot, industrialist and politician, who grew up in the soil, air and water of Odisha, became Biju Babu from Bijayananda Patnaik because of his all this extraordinary persona.

A centenary tribute to the legend…!

2 – How and When Naveen Enter into Politics...?

1946, October 16th. This was the day when father Bijayananda Patnaik and mother Gyan Patnaik's lap was filled with happiness for the third time. There was a wave of happiness flowing in their ancestral house "Anand Bhavan" Cuttack. Because a baby boy was born out of the womb of the great mother Gyan Patnaik.

That day was a historic day for Odisha. Who knew that this little infant sleeping in the cradle would one day write history in Odisha's politics. Perhaps even father Biju Patnaik would not have thought of that, one day his little son would rule Odisha for more than two decades. One day he will change the entire equation of politics in Odisha. Perhaps Biju Babu would not have thought that his beloved son will be so politically capable that for more than two decades he occupied the chair of the Chief Minister of Odisha and will rule in the hearts of 4.5 crores of Odiya.

Mr. Naveen Patnaik is the third child of his parents. His elder brother Prem Patnaik, who is a well-established industrialist in Delhi and elder sister Geeta Mehta is an international well recognized writer. Born in a historic city like Cuttack, Naveen Patnaik has completed his studies from many renowned educational institutions in the country and abroad.

After completing his studies, he had shown a great interest in writing. From 1985 to 1993 he wrote four excellent books. The books written by him are, *Second Paradise, A Desert Kingdom and The Garden of Life.* These books are such books which, besides being very unique in the literature world, have also achieved best seller status. This is shows his love towards writing. The magic hidden in the writings of Naveen Babu is also expressed in his paintings.

He is also a highly skilled painter. An artist with deep passion for art. He has great weakness towards the traditional art of Odisha. The design of *"Krishi Bhawan"*, only government building in the country which has received the world architect award, is Naveen's brainchild.

Father Biju Patnaik was a prominent leader at the national level in the country. He was the Chief Minister of the state twice and many times ministers in the center. He had a lot of influence not only in the state but also in Delhi Politics. But he never allowed his children to enter in politics. He kept his three children far away from politics.

He kept his children away from even the shadow of politics. Biju Babu's three children, two sons and a daughter, are all renowned in their respective fields. No one even knew the names of his children. When the new residence if Biju Babu was ready, its construction was completed and then the house was named as Naveen Nivas.

Naveen Patnaik is the name of Biju Babu's younger son and this house is named after him. Almost no one knew about this at that time. Odisha was unaware about the persona; we Odia were unaware about Naveen Babu.

Because since his childhood Naveen Patnaik had gone far away from the soil and the environment of Odisha. Only a few years, he spent his childhood, did his schooling in St. Josephs Convent in Cuttack.

He had just spent a few years in Odisha during his school life. After that he went to Delhi. He continued his studies in the Prestigious *Welham Boys School* in Dehradun. Then he moved to famous *The Doon School*, Dehradun and there he completed his senior Cambridge certificate at the age of 17. For his bachelor's degree in arts, he attended Kirori Mal College, Delhi University.

Not only this but Naveen has also spent a lot of time in America. He has many renowned and celebrity friends. He loved travelling, he has traveled a lot while living in America with his friends. He has endless love for history, art, literature and athletics. And as a writer, all three books written by him are highly recognized across the world.

Despite being from a distinguished political family, he never seemed to be conscious or interested in politics. He was absolutely happy and was enjoying his glittering party life with his high profile friends in Delhi.

He ran a boutique named Psychedelic in the capital's Oberoi Hotel. He was hosting the high profile friends like musician Mick Jagger, Jacqueline Onassis and also the wife of former US President J.F. Kennedy in his Delhi based Bunglow in APJ Abdul Kalam Marg (Aurangeb Road then).

The lifestyle was completely different there in Lutyens. He was living a very luxurious life there without any bothering. Leave aside interest in Odisha's politics, he never preferred to come Odisha. Forget about reading or writing Odia, he didn't even speak Odia.

Then how did Naveen Babu step into politics?

After crossing 50 years of age, what was the sudden need to enter politics?

How a writer became a successful politician?

That day was April 17th 1997, when the leader of people slept forever. A Great leader passed away. A day when the people of Odisha felt themselves as orphan for the first time. His last rites were performed at the Puri Swargadwara. A sea of people were seen on the sea shore of Puri.

Wherever you look, just only head and head of people. Never before such a huge crowd had gathered in the Puri Swargadwara for anyone's funeral. It would not be a mistake to say that this is also included in a huge record. When Biju Babu's dead body wrapped in the national flags of three countries left for Puri from Bhubaneswar, lakhs of people took part in the precession.

People from every corner of Odisha were coming towards Puri, and the purpose was only to have the last glance of their beloved leader.

An impossible crowd was seen that day. And this was the love and goodness of the entire *"Odisha baashi"* towards Biju Babu.

So this is how Biju Babu's last rites performed. And all the Odisha baasi said goodbye to their Hero, their leader. After this the round of speculation started. That who will be the heir to Biju Babu's political empire. From Bhubaneswar to Delhi, the rounds of meetings started.

When Biju Babu died, he was the MP from Aska constituency Janata Dall.

So, who will inherit his political legacy? Who will contest the by-election on Biju Babu's seat from Aska? Actually, the party heads were looking towards the family first. That Biju Babu's elder son Prem Patnaik will enter in politics. And everyone was expecting the same. That's why party's senior leaders even requested to Prem Babu.

But there was no signal from him. Later Prem Babu clearly told that he is not interested in contesting elections. After this everyone was expecting that Biju Babu's only beloved daughter Gita would enter politics. Gita, who was living in America after her marriage, also flatly refused to join politics and contest the election.

After this the last option was Naveen Babu. No one expected this from Naveen Babu, nicknamed Pappu. That Naveen will ever agree to contest elections. That's why no one thought it necessary to even ask him.

Everyone knew that Naveen will never agree to join politics. Naveen, who do not even talk more with anyone of his father Biju Babu's friends or meet with them. Biju Babu's friends and colleagues who came to his Delhi based Bunglow did not even know Naveen properly. Because many of them neither had ever seen Naveen inside the house nor did Naveen Babu ever meet them.

The rounds of meeting and discussions had intensified that who will contest the by-election from Biju Babu's Aska constituency. The party leaders, high commands of Janata Dall were more worried about this than family. Many types of questions were arising in everyone's mind regarding the by-election, inside and outside the party.

Experts say that everyone's questions, if and but came to an end when Naveen suddenly went to his elder brother Prem Patnaik and elder sister Gita Mehta, both of them were in their residence, APJ Abdul Kalam Marg in Delhi. (Then Aurangzeb road).

If both of you do not want to contest the election, then can I participate in the by-election? Naveen asked permission from his elder brother and elder sister to contest the by-election!

Both Prem Babu and Gita Madam were surprised to hear this from Naveen Babu's mouth. By that time Naveen had written his three books. However, both the siblings were surprised and also very happy at the same time to see Naveen's sudden interest in politics.

Well, whatever it may be, now the exceptional truth was that Naveen had agreed to contest the by-election from Aska constituency. A personality without special interest in politics how far will it go? A man with so much simplicity and soberness, how much success will he get? Many leaders had doubts regarding this. And many leaders were also happy as they can take advantage of the simplicity of Naveen in the future. Finally, Naveen Patnaik was brought to Odisha by plane to contest in election.

When he entered politics 25 years ago. Very few people knew him that time. That day perhaps no one would have guessed that Naveen is going to create a new history in the state politics. After his entry into politics, the entire equation of the state politics had changed.

Naveen, who started his political career as a parliamentarian by winning the by-election from Aska. Now he has more than two decades of state Governance in his hands. In these years, he has turned into a uncontestant politician.

When the architect of modern Odisha Biju Babu left this world forever, that time everyone thought that it was impossible to take his place. Maybe no one knew this that day, the person who have shouldered Biju Babu's funeral pyre. That man Naveen Patnaik one day will carry the banquet of entire Odisha on his shoulder.

After independence, he is one such personality in the state politics who could not be challenged till now. Before 1997, only few people had heard Naveen Babu's name. Naveen was at a considerable distance from Odisha and Odisha's politics.

But after Biju Babu's death, Naveen's life had completely changed. Perhaps Biju Babu's friends were thinking at that time by using Naveen as a pawn, they will move up the political ladder. But after proving them wrong, Naveen built a magnificent political fort for himself.

So, these were few glimpses of Naveen Babu that why he entered into the politics.

How he started a new and wonderful era?

3 – Opponents Said, Naveen Babu Zindabaad

"Tulasi Duyee Potra Ru Baasey". This is a very famous and old saying in Odisha, which means "Basil's seedling spreads its aroma right from the first two leaves".

How and under what circumstances did Naveen Patnaik enter into politics after Biju Babu's death, I tried to describe about this topic a little in the previous chapter. In 1997 Mr. Naveen Patnaik started his political journey from Aska constituency by-election.

That journey too started with a splendid victory by a huge margin. Very quickly Mr. Naveen Patnaik became a member of parliament after winning the by-election to Aska constituency and then he got re-elected to parliament twice in quick succession.

When the national democratic alliance (NDA) led by Prime Minister Atal Bihari Vajpayee came to power in 1998, Naveen became a union minister.

He remained a union minister when Vajpayee took oath as Prime Minister again the following year.

Meanwhile, he also started looking into the political situation of his state, Odisha. Of course, Naveen came into politics only for the shake of his state. He came into politics only for the people of his state. The concerns of his people bound to bring him into politics.

That's why within a few months of entering into politics, Biju Janata Dal (BJD) was formed as the regional party of Odisha. Named after the legendary former Chief Minister and soft architect of modern Odisha. 26th December 1997 was the auspicious day on which the party was formed with deep rooted belief in secularism and value based politics, and exemplary commitment to the development of Odisha.

The purpose of Biju Janata Dal's formation was only and only the welfare of the people of Odisha. The basic and only aim of Mr. Naveen

Patnaik and BJD was to regain their lost identity and give a new identity to the backward state into a developed state. Which was also Biju Babu's dream to seeing Odisha in the queue of developing states of the country.

And then the Biju Janata Dal started its glorious journey. Under the leadership of Naveen Patnaik, BJD was busy in winning every election one after the other. Be it Lok Sabha election, Assembly election or urban local bodies elections. The BJD has not looked back yet.

The party has won every election in the state since 2000 and Naveen himself entered the state assembly by winning from the very challenging Hinjili Constituency in 2000, which was not easy at all that time. But it was as if Naveen had set out on a mission.

How could anyone stop him from victory?

How could anything become an obstacle in the path of Naveen Patnaik, who have to take political decisions of the fate of Odisha for decades? Naveen's hard work and strong willpower paid off and he got a great and splendid victory.

It seemed as if the crown of Chief Minister of Odisha was really waiting for Naveen. Finally, not only he entered in the Odisha assembly as legislature member but also in the year 2000, Naveen took oath as the Chief Minister of Odisha for the first time.

But before entering into state politics the cleverness and success with which he had successfully removed his biggest rival within the party, Vijay Mohapatra from the way. That was an extraordinary and unimaginable political step by Naveen Patnaik. This single move had created a stir in the state politics.

This one move was enough to create terror in the opposition camp. Whether inside the party or outside the party, the opponents had come to know that whom they were considering as a small child in politics, thinking him innocent. This was their big mistake. They were considering him as a fool. Those who were optimistic that Naveen's simplicity could be used as a ladder to achieve their own interests.

They all were proven wrong and understood their own exact place, where to be and where to stand.

The way Naveen removed Vijay Mohapatra from his path by political moves even before the game started. People are still in shock and curious that how it happened? That one move was enough to prove that how much politics was ingrained in Naveen. That is why it is said that "*Tulasi Duyee Potra Ru Baasey*". Basil leaves does not need to be old to give its fragrance, two tinny leaves are enough to prove how fragrant it is…!

After occupying the Chief Ministerial chair. One by one he had shown the way to out from party to his opponent inside the party. Leave aside giving any kind of support or encourage to corruption and evil, he did not tolerate it even a pinch at all.

No matter who it is. May it be MLA or Minister, Member of Parliament or Member of Rajya Sabha, bureaucrats or any class officer, he never compromised even for a moment. Naveen created a clean image of himself by placing a black blanket of filth over his opponents face. And with this his tremendous popularity also increased day by day.

It is not just that Naveen expelled his rival from the party on the strength of his political astuteness. His greatness, cleverness and extraordinary leadership talent are not limited to just this. The condition of Odisha and Odisha's politics was so shattered and painful, when Naveen entered politics. Corruption had reached its peak.

There were a lot of political instability in the state. The Chief Minister had changed thrice in five years of the same party. The health of the state was going through its worst phase. Corruption was badly spreading. In such a situation, when Naveen entered the politics of the state, he started his journey with only one intention and one mindset only that he will only work for Odisha and Odia people's welfare and progress.

We know everything that what Naveen did for his people after becoming the Chief Minister of Odisha, but before becoming the Chief Minister he had clearly proved his intentions, he had made his visions clear even before sitting on the Chief Ministers' chair.

How can anyone even forget about the super cyclone of 1999? What kind of attack did it inflict on the Odisha's residents which can never be forgotten?

Even after two decades, people have not been able to forget the great Holocaust. Even today tears roll down from eyes when they think about that day. According to government figures, more than 10,000 people died due to wind blowing at a speed of 250 kilometers per hour. Non-Government figures are much higher than this.

Due to this super cyclone, a large amount of flood water had also entered inside. Lakhs of people were left homeless and injured. At one place if his young son drowned in front of a father, husband drowned in front of her wife at another place and somewhere son in front of mother. But those people could not do anything even after so much efforts. Coastal district of Odisha had the maximum damage due to super cyclone.

The death toll of more than 8000 was crossed in Jagatsinghpur district alone. From this you can imagine how terrible and dangerous this super cyclone was. The sea water was pushed forward for approximately 8-9 kilometers. Due to which the scene of this disaster became more heart wrenching. Lakhs of people became homeless, because of which they had to live in tents for years.

According to a report, property worth of $4.44 billion were destroyed. Out of this mostly the farming sector of Odisha was affected. Not only the government of India but also the foreign countries had helped Odisha that time.

The situation had become such worst that no one had any hope that Odisha would be able to stand back ever again. Odisha was completely flattered. Firstly, the economic condition of Odisha was already not good and to top it the hit of this super cyclone. Political instability was also sprinkling petrol to the fire.

That time Giridhar Gamang was the Chief Minister of the state. The condition of the state was beyond his control. The situation became so panic and uncontrollable that he had to resign from the Chief Ministers position. The government was not at all prepared to face such natural disaster. And then after Mr. Gamang resigns, Mr. Hemananda Biswal took over as the Chief Minister.

In such situation, Naveen was a minister in the center at that time. Newly entered into politics.

At a time when senior and veteran leaders of a party like congress had laid down their weapons. What could a newly established party like BJD and newly joined politician Naveen would do at that time?

But even though he had no role in the state politics, Naveen made a lot of efforts for its upliftment.

Senior editor, Mr. Prahallad Singh says about Naveen Patnaik's personal and political life that Naveen today has made his name on the record of India's second longest reigning CM tour and very soon that means if he wins the coming 2024 election and again becomes CM then he will become India's first CM to stay for the longest period.

Today he is known as the second longest serving CM in India but very soon Naveen Babu will take over the first place. Naveen has achieved one record after another. What is the root cause behind this?

Mr. Prahallad Singh reveals in a private news channel's interview about Naveen and his unbreakable records. He says that the simplicity, the innocence within Naveen and his framework for working is very unique and different from others. And if we will focus on his personal life, which is completely common. Meaning, some people were thinking of politics as a business.

But after Naveen Babu entered into politics, from 1997 to till date, no one will ever be able to say that Naveen used politics as business. No one can ever say that by investing in politics, he has done anything for himself, for his family or for his future.

Till date, not a single personal allegation has been leveled against him in the last 26 years. Out of which he served as a minister at the center for 3 years and as the Chief Minister of the state for more than 23 years. Naveen Babu never thought of politics as a source of earning money or had any such greed, he did not even try.

He doesn't have such desire nor insistence towards this. This is his life and this is how he is living and want to live. And this his modus operandi. Because of all these things, the public has developed a very strong faith in him. A love is born in everyone's heart for him. To understand this well, Mr. Prahallad Singh also shared a small story of his past experience with Naveen Babu. And he said that;

At the time of 1999 super cyclone, Prahallad Babu says that he was engaged in the relief work at that time in Ersama. As we know, Naveen's government was not formed in Odisha that time. He was a minister at the center then. Naveen Babu had come to Bhubaneswar at that time. Suddenly one day Naveen Babu called him (to Prahallad Singh) and he reached near Naveen Babu at the earliest. The relief work was going on very speedily.

Especially in Ersama area, relief work was being done very fast and on a large scale. Ersama was one of the most affected areas of Jagatsinghpur due to the super cyclone. Naveen Babu did query about all the works related to relief from Prahallad, how is relief distribution work going on etc.

He was briefing from Prahallad. Then Naveen asked Prahallad Singh that if you need anything else then tell me.

Prahallad Singh said that there are many needs but for now the biggest need is that to revise the health system which has been completely paralyzed in the Ersama area, 24-25 doctors had come from Sevagram Medical Collage. Their living arrangements have been made at a far distance from Ersama. Due to which they have to face a lot of troubles and also waste of time. Due to this, their work also got hampered.

"If you had arranged for a vehicle, it would have been very easy for them to travel and work." Mr. Prahallad said to Naveen Babu.

After hearing this from Mr. Prahallad, Naveen Babu immediately arranged two trekkers car for them and that too for six months.

"Today the topic came out and I got a chance to tell this here today, otherwise Naveen Babu won't even remember this." Mr. Prahallad Singh said.

And my purpose to remembering this matter is, I just want to say that even before he became the Chief Minister, how much love and concern he had for his people. And the situation in which he became the Chief Minister after Super Cyclone, this thing is not hidden from anyone. The foundation of his government was laid during the devastated condition of Odisha.

"That time Naveen Babu's only concern was how Odisha would be transformed into a developed state in India. For that he continued doing various types of ventures. Even before he sworn as the Chief Minister of Odisha, his concern and effort for Odisha's people is always in his priority list." Mr. Singh said.

Whether Naveen Babu remains in power or not, the main subject of his concern has been only and only 4.5 crores Odia's development. Just like Biju Babu's way of concern was. Biju Babu, for whom my people, my language, my soil and my state used to be dominant.

Whether he was in power or not. Power had never been able to create any hindrances in his stream of worries. In the same way, in 1999 cyclone, Naveen did not look for any excuse to serve his people despite not being in power.

Just like Biju Babu was always moving forward towards his goal. Power has never conspired for Biju Babu. Naveen Babu has also followed the footsteps of his father Mr. Biju Patnaik." Mr. Prahallad Singh said.

Mr. Prahallad Singh further says; when he became Chief Minister in 2000 with lots of concerned about how Odisha would be developed. Under this concerns he tie-up with BJP, till 2008 both ran the government jointly. But when BJP gave up, he repeats BJP had given up, Naveen did not leave BJP. BJP not only left BJD's hand but they demanded Naveen's resignation in front of Governor House along with Congress.

"At that time when adverse circumstances came, he as a man became strong. Because of him coming in that adverse circumstances, BJD became more strong and powerful. Naveen Babu got more strength. Due to the same strength and power, he was able to win the hearts of the people all over Odisha. Because of winning the hearts of his people, Naveen Babu became more powerful and continued to work further." Mr. Prahallad Singh said.

When we are discussing the concept of development. So, the word *"Development"* can mean to different for different people. But for Naveen the meaning of development is his decisions taken keeping in mind for the combined development of 4.5 crores of Odia. No discrimination of any kind based on caste, religion, Color or any other differences.

In the past 24-25 years during his tenure as Chief Minister, in the last five terms. There will be no such segment, there won't be any such person or there will be no such organization, leaving aside whom, Odisha would have been thinking about moving forward.

This is the beauty of Naveen Babu's developed concern stream. We all are aware about *"Mission Shakti"*. The most popular scheme made with 70 lakhs women. Now a day, political parties are worried about letting the women of Mission Shakti stay in the village, let them stay at home, doing dirty politics regarding them. But Naveen Babu's aim is to make them self-reliant, to empower them from an economic point of view and also from a social point of view.

When 70 lakhs women will become stronger and emerge from the village level to front level then just think about where Odisha's situation will reach after 13 years. When we will be celebrating the 100th anniversary of the formation of Odisha. That time after 13 years, what extent would Odisha will be looking strong and empowered. This is a bit difficult for us to think about but such way of thinking, such futuristic thought is full inside Mr. Naveen Patnaik.

The power to take decisions like this, the ability to such thinking and understanding is filled in great abundance inside Naveen Babu. These were some beautiful thoughts and glimpses of making beautiful decisions.

Today Mr. Naveen Patnaik has completed more than 26 years of joining politics. He was a minister at the center for 3 years and then more than 23 years of experience as the Chief Minister of the state.

Today he is the longest serving Chief Minister of Odisha. Today he has all types of power, political power, economic power, administrative power etc. All types of resources are under his control. Economically, the state is in a very good position. It would not be a mistake if we say that there is no opposition in the politics of the state.

But, what did Naveen had in his hands when he entered politics? Had nothing…!

Only and only strong will power. The sole aim was to see Odisha as developed state in the country. And by transforming into a developed state the dream to see himself and his people in the queue of developed state of India.

Naveen was so concerned about this thought and dreams that he was involved in every matter personally. He himself kept an eye on every issue and made notes himself.

Mr. Debasis Nayak, one of the founding face of BJD. Debasis Babu, once known as one of the very important person to Mr. Naveen Patnaik. Mr. Debasis Nayak says in an interview to a private channel.

"When Naveen Babu used to go for campaigning or he used to go for any inquiry about some project or work. In those initial days, Naveen himself used to write down everything with a pen and paper. And then later he himself used to follow up the work. Whether the work was done or not, he was not leaving in peace to the officers or the people who are responsible?"

"Naveen Babu always used to check his check list himself, what work has been done and what work is left? In 1997, at that time when this journey was started, we did not know that Naveen Babu would be the Chief Minister or he will remain 23-24 years continuously in power. But he had only and only craziness for work. Even if we finished work at 1:00 in the night and went to the guest house and then again Naveen Babu used to call us early in the morning at 4:00 and wake us up."

He used to check himself whether we got up or not, whether the work started or not? He himself kept checking. Mr. Debasis Nayak says that there was a feeling of satisfaction in his heart while working with Mr. Naveen Patnaik. And we felt good that we were working with a good man, with a man of responsibility, a person with integrity and honesty. We felt very proud to work with Naveen Babu. Mr. Nayak said.

Mr. Debasis says, Naveen Babu believes only in work. He never ran for power or authority. Naveen Babu had suffered a lot in his early political days. With great sincerity he was looking forward. At that time, he had always lack of money also.

There was a time, when he even spent his royalties, earnings from his books for public works. Used to roam from place to place in a broken car. Debasis Babu says, "Once it happened that when we were going somewhere for an important work and the car ran out of petrol on the way. Then somehow petrol was arranged and we set out for our work.

It took about 40-45 minutes to arrange petrol and the whole time Naveen Babu was standing on the road. Without any hesitation or complain. This is his character, very simple and different".

Naveen Babu used to remember even small incidents so deeply that it seemed very beautiful. Recalling an incident, Debasis Babu says that, "At that time, whenever Naveen Babu used to go out in his car, a man used to stand on the way with his bullet. As soon as Naveen Babu's car passed, that man used greet with folded hand and then he goes away. This had become that man's usual routine.

Later I also got shocked that how does he know, when and what time Naveen Babu's car will go out. Although I never even paid attention to this. But once we were going somewhere, I was in the car with Naveen Babu and when our car reached near the roundabout, that man was standing there with his bullet in the same spot. And as soon as he saw his car, he folded his hands and greeted Naveen Babu as per his routine".

He continued, "On seeing him, Naveen Babu also waved his hand towards him and quickly told me, Debasis Babu look at this man. He is my lucky man. Whenever we go out, I find this man standing here and wishing us. And then after that I looked at the man and I thought oh yes that's right. And I also wondered how he knew what time we would leave.

Well, that is a different matter but I found this love and affection of Naveen Babu towards a common man very beautiful. That Naveen Babu considers an ordinary common man as his lucky man. Naveen Babu is a very sensitive man. He pays attention to his responsibilities with full dedication". Mr. Debasis Nayak said.

Mr. Debasis Nayak further says; when there was a severe water shortage in the Aska constituency. He had brought Antalu from Gujarat at his own expense. Antulu, also known as waterman. Work was going on regarding where good water will come out. Naveen Babu was so serious and worried about this water problem which is so admirable.

That he himself stood there under a tree without eating or drinking anything for a whole day and kept watching the work. He himself stood under the tree and got the water bore well digging work done. He is a hard task master. He never chose the shortcut or easy path. Naveen Babu always wanted to achieve on the basis of his strong determination and hard work.

If you look back, the Hinjili has never been easy or positive for us or our party. Even during Biju Babu's time also, I (Mr. Debasis Nayak) had 5k minus. Apart from Hinjili of Aska constituency, we were successful everywhere else. But Naveen Babu chose Hinjili. If he had stood from anywhere else, he would have won the election comfortably.

But he chose Hinjili only. He had chosen Hinjili as a challenge. After that we went to the people of Hinjili there. Naveen Babu himself checked the issues, tried to find out what the problems are there by himself. Made people believe that he would solve their problems. He roamed around place to place himself. Worked hard day and night.

"Then the people there were bound to accept Naveen Babu. Then the people there blessed Naveen Babu with their blessings. Then Hinjili became the bastion of victory for Mr. Naveen Patnaik. And then a place like Hinjili became positive for Naveen Babu, for us and our party. Such is Naveen Babu's personality. The owner of a very soft, loyal, generous and beautiful personality". Mr. Debasis Nayak said.

That's why even I could not stop my pen from writing "*Naveen Babu Zindabaad*"!

Let's go little further…! And let's try to find out whether we have committed any mistake by writing this…?

Two decades ago, a young man on whom Mr. Naveen Patnaik had made a prediction, today it has been proven accurate.

In 2000, when BJP and BJD formed an alliance, they decided to contest the election jointly. Pallahara, an assembly constituency in the central Angul District. From Pallahara Dharmendra Pradhan was contesting assembly election for the first time in 2000.

Dharmendra Pradhan, son of the then union minister of state for surface transport, Mr. Debendra Pradhan. Dharmendra Pradhan was an activist of the BJP's student wing. The Akhil Bharatiya Vidyarthi Parishad (ABVP) and former student union leader of Utkal University. Dharmendra was a little known figure in 2000. Ambitious and strong.

Naveen Babu was sitting in silence in a worried state and was listening carefully the election results announcements. Results were coming one after another from different constituencies. Who won which seat, and who lead on which seat?

Meanwhile, when Naveen Babu heard this voice, that BJP's Dharmendra Pradhan has won from Pallahara. That time suddenly one line came out from his mouth. *"Oh' I've got a problem"*. This statement came out of Naveen's mouth with shock and surprise. Mr. Ruben Banerjee reveal in his book 'NAVEEN PATNAIK'.

BJP and BJD was alliance that time and they were contesting the election jointly. Dharmendra was the candidate of BJP. Then why did Naveen Babu use this sentence at that time. Maybe that time no one understood this shocking sentence of Mr. Naveen Patnaik. But today Naveen's farsightedness is clearly visible. He had demonstrated his political wisdom, his political concerns, his political thought that time only.

Today it is understandable after decades. Of course, at that time Naveen himself also entered new in politics. But still he had proved at that very moment that *"Tulasi Duyee Patra Ru Baasey"*. Maybe, it takes too long to understand this. Because today, Mr. Dharmendra Pradhan is Naveen Babu's biggest rival in state politics. By the way, opposition's situation in Odisha's politics is almost mean to know.

Still, people believe that after leaving Mr. Naveen Patnaik in Odisha today's date, if there is any CM face in Odisha's politics then he is Mr. Dharmendra Pradhan of BJP. If reports are to be believe then Mr. Dharmendra Pradhan is the CM face from BJP now in Odisha. So, this is the same day and this is the same face about which Naveen Babu had portrayed 20 years ago that this face will one day stand in front of me as my biggest rival in politics.

Anyway, our purpose in telling such old and important information at this point of time is that, this is rarely seen in today's cutthroat politics that your biggest rival is saying two good words about you!

But here with Naveen Babu, something is different and extraordinary. He is such a personality that of course his fans are fans, even Naveen's opponents also do not hold back in praising him.

Mr. Dharmendra Pradhan, Education Minister in center in the NDA Government. CM face of BJP in Odisha. Biggest opponent of Mr. Naveen Patnaik. Dharmendra Babu says in ANI's Editor Smita Prakash's one show that Naveen Babu is very true gentleman, a splendid leader and I don't have any objection or hesitation to acknowledge this about him.

Dharmendra Babu further say, "Very few people get this kind of opportunity in a democracy. Respected Jyoti Basu ji got this opportunity and Mr. Pawan Chamlin ji has got this and today Naveen Babu has got this wonderful opportunity in Odisha. I am happy for him.

People's trust is the biggest thing in democracy. And I have no objection in saying that BJP is the number two party in Odisha. According to local level, BJP is the opponent party of BJD. Actually, the thing is that the trust that the Odia people have on Naveen Babu because of his refined personality. That's why such a large amount of people's wave of trust comes on him. Naveen Babu is a very decent man. His way of doing politics is unique. He doesn't believe in being aggressive or abusive in politics. But it is very unfortunate in today's politics that we have chosen being abusive as a way of opposing. But it is different in case of Naveen Babu. He has a parameter and he does politics within that parameter.

Being a decent and sensitive man. Whatever the matter is, whether he have consent or unconsent, he works according to his parameter. People say that he is not aggressive, not abusive. I believe that people like him for this very reason. His calm and unique nature attracts people. So, these were few words of our Central Education Minister, Mr. Dharmendra Pradhan. The biggest opponents of BJD and of course Naveen Patnaik's too".

So, as I said, it is very rare that your opponents praise you. Supporters of a leader praises him or express their support by saying long live him (*Zindabaad*). That's very common and usual but if your opponents saying "*Naveen Babu Zindabaad*", then its beyond everything…!

When your opponent, sing your praising, appreciate your work. This praise is incredible. This *Zindabaad* is very much appreciated. So, when Naveen's biggest opponent Mr. Dharmendra Pradhan praised Naveen Babu in a public forum, counted his personality, his work, this event takes a public to an another level. Indeed, it is also a big achievement in the list of success of Naveen Babu that his opponent is praising him.

Looking at the beautiful relationship between the ruling party and the opposition party, I also could not stop my pen from writing "*Naveen Babu Zindabaad*"!

In fact, it should be like this in a healthy democracy that the good deeds of the ruling party for the people should be praised and the wrong deeds should be criticized and not to be glorified. The entire system of governance should be "of the people, for the people, by the people". As said by *Abraham Lincoln*. That's the beauty of democracy.

4 – 5T-Initiative

Now a day, wherever you will go in Odisha, you will definitely hear the word mostly everywhere!

You will face this word in excessive quantity!

And the name of that word is 5T. If you go to school there you will find 5T, if you go to hospital there is 5T and if you go to stadium there also you will get to face 5T.

5T, 5T, 5T

What exactly is this 5T?

What is the meaning of 5T?

What is the importance of 5T and how it works exactly?

To what extent is this useful and beneficial for Odisha people?

We will try to know some very important facts, truth and benefits about this 5T.

Well, it's not about today. Even before becoming CM, he had told, he had cleared his intentions, he made clear the purpose of entering politics. Not coming to amass wealth for himself or any of his family members. He had expressed his wishes even before becoming CM that he is coming into politics only and only for his people, only to serve his people. Nothing else.

Mr. Naveen Patnaik, has been innovative in his approach in running the government in a very transparent manner since assuming power in march 2000. Mr. Naveen Patnaik is known for many innovative schemes that are tailor-made for different needs of the people.

"Mo Sarkar" is a governance program. The "Mo Sarkar" initiative is seen as a way to shift power away from the bureaucracy back to the people and make governance more evidence-based, efficient, and equitable. 5T is a "Mo Sarkar" initiative program by the Government of Odisha to serve the people of Odisha a good governance and to provide a good governance policy. To judge the work properly in government offices, the Odisha government introduces this 5T. In this 5T program the 5T stands as 5 pillars

1st T for – Transparency

2nd T for – Technology

3rd T for – Teamwork

4th T for - Time

5th T for – Transformation

The vision of The Hon'ble Chief Minister Mr. Naveen Patnaik, behind the establishment of 5T;

The four and half crore people of Odisha, have once again blessed us with an opportunity to serve them. I am eternally indebted to the people for the faith they have reposed in us.

*I would like to emphasize once again on the 3Ts of governance- **Teamwork, transparency** and **Technology** leading to **transformation**.*

I am going to add a fifth dimension to this– Time.

Time is of critical essence. The youth of today are in a hurry–

If we could get an international recognition in FANI – it's because of timely evacuation.

If we could do Asian Athletic Championship in 90 days.

If we could bring 30 lakhs more women into the Mission Shakti fold.

If we could roll out KALIA – an initiative nationally applauded in 15 days.

If we could ground near universal health coverage – Biju Swasthya Kalyan Yojana in 30 days.

This is the pace that people want in their governance model.

Today we have approved in principal the party manifesto as priority of government. 365 days from now – On 29th may 2020 we shall present before the people our achievements visa-vis promises. I know some of the promises take time. I want the council of Ministers to put their best efforts in this regard. I want all of us to focus on transformation towards a new Odisha.

> ➤ *An Empowered Odisha – where poverty will be a thing of past*
> ➤ *An Empowered Odisha – where women are equal partners in growth and development*
> ➤ *An Empowered Odisha – which is inclusive of all vulnerable sections in its landscape of development.*
> ➤ *An Empowered Odisha – where dreams of our youth come true.*

The world should know that's Odisha time has come…! And Our Time Starts Now.

Mr. Naveen Patnaik

Hon'ble Chief Minister, Odisha

Let's understand the 5T pillars;

1st Pillar – Transparency = Transparency means that while government work is done by government officials, the project should be done with the complete honesty and openness. Common people can see and can get information about it, which is their right of course. And if injustice is done to them then common people could be able to give their feedback to government and government officials.

So that the government can take action. Transparency is the biggest powerful factor of 5Ts program. And it is a crucial element of 5T initiative. This includes providing easy access to information, reducing bureaucratic red tape and promoting ethical and accountable conduct within the government.

2nd Pillar – Technology = Technology refers to methods, systems, devises. Which is used for practical purposes in our daily life. Earlier to store any kind of Data, we used to use pen and paper. But now a day we use computers to store any Data.

By using technology in any type of work, it requires less effort and less time. And it provides high accuracy of information. So that is why adopting technology more and more in every field is the 2nd T included in the 5T initiative. And the government is encouraging everyone to use technology.

3rd Pillar – Teamwork = Simply meaning of teamwork is working together of people to achieve a certain goal or to complete a task in the most effective and efficient way. Teamwork has played a very important role to function properly for any organization and institution. Teamwork makes any work easier and faster. In this perspective *Teamwork* is included in the 5T.

4th Pillar – Time = Time played a vital role in our life. To complete any specified work within a particular *time* period with full dedication and hard work, *Time* is being included in the 5T charter.

5th Pillar – Transformation = The last one is transformation. A complete or major changes in someone's or something's appearance or instance. For example, everyone knows what was the school condition in Odisha earlier, mostly in the rural areas. Poor classrooms, broken furniture in classes and offices, without any playground or garden, even proper toilet was not available in the most of the schools in Odisha.

Forget about the library and computer labs, most of the schools were deprived of even minimum facilities. But the way schools have been transformed because of this 5T transformation program of Naveen Government. Like, digital classroom, e-library, garden, playground, proper toilet, new modern furniture etc. this is called transformation.

To provide quality and productive education in Odisha, the school transformation program is introduced by the Chief Minister Mr. Naveen Patnaik. Which comes under the 5T. Mr. Naveen Patnaik wished that students of Odisha should excel in every field, know about new technology and bring glory to the state.

As part of High School Transformation program the existing old schools have been renovated. The old furniture of the schools has been replaced with new modern furniture. Brighter lighting system has been installed in the class room. Which helps to illuminate teaching space. Audio visual teaching and projector also has been installed in the class rooms.

Which helps to teach, to learn the process effectively. And students will stay active in their studies, will be able to build interest, will be able to become a good observer. New science laboratories have been provided for students to conduct experiments. E-library facilities for reading Nobel and other scholarly books have been provided to the schools under 5T school transformation program.

The Hon'ble Chief Minister Mr. Naveen Patnaik says that "Through this school transformation program the discrimination between private and government schools has been reduced. And students are finding an environment of private school in their village". Mr. Patnaik also said, "5T school transformation program has eliminated the difference between school in the city and in the villages.

The facilities which was available only in schools of big towns, that will also be available in village schools too. It is the common responsibilities of all of us to help the students realize their dreams. They should have a big goal or aim in their life. Work hard to reach their goal".

And whatever the challenges will come in life, they will face them with confidence and will achieve their goals successfully. This is the objective of school transformation.

In the first phase of school transformation total 1075 schools are being transformed in 30 districts. And current details about total school transformation is that more than 6,872 of schools were transformed by march 2023 under the 5T initiative. As a result, private schools had 16,05,000 students in 2019-20, but the number of students has been reduced to 14,62,000 in 2021-22. Which implies that number of students enrolled in government schools have increased.

So, over all we can say that by using technology in any type of work, by everyone's co-operation and collaboration, by doing team work, by managing time with transparency in the entire system, and to bring total system transformation within the time limit is what we call as 5T.

5T action plan approved by the Hon'ble CM Mr. Naveen Patnaik for Higher Education Departments is to ensure better service delivery to public in Higher Education Sector. So, Technology, Teamwork, Transparency, Time and Transformation are the five factors on which performance of Government officials and projects will be judged.

Well, if we are talking about 5T and how can it be possible that there is no mentioning of Mr. VK Pandian. Odisha has more than 200 serving IAS officers, but only one of them is hogging all the headlines. Yes, V.Karthikeyan Pandian, the 2000 batch IAS officer hails from Tamil Nadu. He began his career as an IAS (Indian Administrative Service) officer in the Punjab cadre.

But his career took a significant turn when he got Odisha cadre by virtue of his marriage to Odia IAS officer, Sujata Rout.

He started his career as Dharmagarh sub-collector in Kalahandi district in 2002 and subsequently assumed district magistrate of Mayurbhanj and Ganjam before his posting in CMO. Later he joined the Odisha CMO in 2011 and became the most trusted lieutenant of Naveen Patnaik. As a collector, his effort to simplify processes in issuance of certificates for people with disabilities was widely recognized.

Mr. Pandian's most prominent role as a bureaucrat was serving as the private secretary to Mr. Naveen Patnaik. He held this position for over a decade. Mr. VK Pandian had his imprint in all key flagship government programs which the Biju Janata Dal Government highlighted as its achievements.

The school transformation, temple renovation, turning Odisha into a sports hub and swiftness in execution of government programs are said to be the brainchild of Mr. Pandian. And now he is serving as the Chairman of 5T initiative and Naveen Odisha scheme, holding a cabinet minister's rank. So, in this way Mr. VK Pandian has a big role behind the success of 5T initiative.

Naveen Patnaik's 5T initiative for good governance in Odisha: A published report about 5T initiative in FRONTLINE, The Hindu.

Hon'ble Chief Minister Naveen Patnaik has been innovative in his approach in running the government in a transparent manner since assuming power in March 2000. He is known for many innovative schemes that are tailor-made for different needs of the people.

In his fifth term as Chief Minister, he has improved upon his previous agenda known as 3T—Teamwork, Transparency and Technology—and created the 5T model of "transparency, teamwork, technology and timeliness leading to transformation" in order to make the governance mechanism citizen-centric.

As a result, Odisha has undertaken key initiatives for implementing citizen-centric good governance over the past few years, with the 5T being at the core of the model. In the Good Governance Index 2021 brought out by the Centre, the State ranks first in two categories—human resource development, and economic governance in the category of group B States. Further, the State has improved its GGI score from 4.44 in 2019 to 4.85 in 2021.

The state ensures time-bound delivery of public services through the legal framework of Odisha Right to Public Services Act, which enables citizens to demand public services as a right. The 'Odisha One' portal is an integrated service delivery framework for over 440 government services across 44 departments at present.

Further, in order to reduce compliance burden for citizens in availing themselves of government services, the state has undertaken major e-governance transformation 5T initiatives in sectors such as education, telecom, cyber security, public grievance redress, tourism, investment and trade, land records and disaster management.

The transformational initiatives are carried out under the active supervision of Mr. VK Pandian, secretary to Chief Minister (5T). Be it makeover of high schools, hospitals, stadiums or restoration of major pilgrimage sites, Mr. Pandian visits different parts of the state and the projects are prepared and implemented with Naveen Patnaik's approval.

The overall improvement in governance mechanism through the transformative 5T model has made Odisha a top destination for new investments. The state was able to attract new investments of over Rs. 2 lakh crore across multiple sectors even during the COVID-19 pandemic. The electronic and Information Technology Department has turned into a critical enabler for ensuring citizen-centric governance to deliver citizen services at the doorsteps of the people.

Naveen Patnaik added the 'Mo Sarkar' initiative to the 5T governance model on Gandhi Jayanti Day in 2019. As part of this, the administration gathers feedback from people visiting different government offices, hospitals and police stations and takes follow-up action.

The Chief Minister, Ministers, the Chief Secretary, Secretaries and other senior officers contact people by phone to get their feedback. The phone numbers of the people who come to government departments are collected randomly with the purpose of improving the governance system.

At a function for the inclusion of different government departments in the Mo Sarkar initiative, Naveen Patnaik said: "The common man must feel empowered. The common man must feel that he is the master. He must feel he is living in a truly democratic system. I myself have made several phone calls and received good feedback. We have taken tough action, wherever there have been lapses and appreciated wherever the feedback has been good".

He went on to say that the success of Mo Sarkar solely depends on the effectiveness of the feedback mechanism. The government has given compulsory retirement to many police officials, doctors and engineers whose track record received negative feedback.

Naveen Patnaik also included COVID-19 management in the Mo Sarkar program to get feedback from patient and front-line workers with regard to improving the management of the situation. Pandian said at the inclusion function that government officials must remember that the dignity of a person coming to a government office is of utmost importance and that this cannot be compromise at any coast.

The 5T initiative backed by Mo Sarkar has proved to be a boon for the people of the state.

Courtesy: FRONTLINE, The Hindu
Prafulla Das, Published: May 09, 2022

5 – Heart Winning Welfare Schemes

Odisha, A state of Art, Culture and Religion. For which we all feel proud. But why was Odisha always mentioned among the poorest states of the country.

There is no shortage of any kind of resources in Odisha. First of all, this state with a manpower of more than 4.5 crores has coastline of 480 kilometers, dams, highly rich in minerals, no shortage of natural resources, fine greenery, fertile agricultural land, weather condition, and there is no shortage of talent as well.

You will definitely find Odias in every field in the country. Mills, Hotels, Industries, IT sector, Banking. We definitely have skills to work in every field. From a simple daily laborer to Reserve Bank of India's Governor, Mr. Shaktikanta Das. Country's first citizen, the woman holding the highest position in the country. Droupadi Murmu, Hon'ble President of India is from Odisha. We have made our presence felt everywhere.

If we talk or think about resources, then Odisha will be counted as a prosperous state. There is no shortage of water, land, forest and mineral resources. Let's understand in short details about the natural resources of Odisha.

If we start from our water resources, many small and big rivers flow here in Odisha. The most prominent among these rivers is the 858 km long Mahanadi. The Hirakud Dam in Sambalpur is on this river. And the construction of this Dam has been finished not today but in 1953. There is Indravati Dam in Jaipur, which is built on the Mahanadi river itself. Along with Mahanadi, Odisha also has rivers like Subarnarekha, Jhabalanga, Baitarini, Brahmini and Rushikulya. So, there is no shortage of water at all.

After water resources, if we look at land resources then we will find here in Odisha most of the land is fertile and useful. Odisha receives rain fall from Northwest as well as South East monsoon. Along with that Odisha's geographical location supports almost all types of forest. Our state Odisha has a 32% forest cover on its entire geographical area. One of the most prominent source of forest in the country. Prominent trees like, Teak, Sal, Shisu, Khaira and Bamboo are found in Odisha.

If we talk about the mineral resources of Odisha, then here is a huge reserve of minerals and energy resources. Like Iron Ore, Manganese, Chromite, Bauxite and limestone are found in large quantities in various parts of Odisha.

If we compare the total mineral resources reserve of the entire country, then India's total 28% of Iron Ore, 24% of Coal, 59% of Bauxite, 98% of Chromite is reserved in Odisha only. Not only in India, Odisha has the world's fourth largest reserve of Bauxite. Not only this, precious stones like China Clay, Fire Clay, Limestone, Quartz, Graphite, Vanadium are also found in Odisha. Then why…???

What was the reason that even after so many years of independence, Odisha was in such a poor condition?

Why did people die out of hunger here?

What was its root cause?

Whom should we blame for poverty and hunger?

From 1947 till 2000, within a total of 53 years, only congress ruled the state for 40 years. India's total mineral's 24% is reserve in Odisha only. And the worst part is that Gujarat and Maharashtra were developing by taking steel and Iron from Odisha. But Odisha was going below the poverty line every day. Starvation was increasing.

The condition of the economy of our state was worsening day by day. But our politicians were busy in conducting elections without any concern. According to the data, elections have been held 22 times from 1947 to 2000.

According to the report on an average in every 2.4 years CM have been changed. And few CM could not complete even one year. So, how can a state develop where there is so much political instability.

But today the situation has changed to a great extent. The state used to be the poorest state in the country 20 years ago. That state is growing today faster than the speed of national growth rate. Where a few years ago some people used to die out of hunger, today the state is not known for starvation but for highest rice production.

The state which was called the poorest state in the country, today spending Rs. 2500 crore in building sports infrastructure and national sports sponsorship.

According to the economic survey in the year 2000, Odisha's poverty rate was approximately 47.15%. At the same time in 2000 the national poverty rate was 26%. This meant Odisha's poverty rate was double to the national poverty.

After 10 years Odisha's poverty rate was 29.9% and national poverty rate was 21.9%. That means, within 10 years, Odisha had reduced its poverty rate by 20% and reached close to national poverty rate.

According to NITI Aayog's NPI report, the poverty is 15%, the NITI Aayog has made the data published with reference to the financial years of 2019-2021. This means that after exactly 10 years the poverty rate in Odisha has reached 15.68%. The national poverty rate average of 2023 is 14.96%, this means Odisha has touched the national average rate. This means that within 20 years, Odisha has reduced its poverty rate from 50% to 15%. And not only poverty, all the poverty index requirement of National Multidimensional, Health, Education and standard of living also has been improved.

The poorest state 20 years ago has today become the fastest growing economy of the country. And it is going faster than India's average growth rate.

But how was this possible?

What is the reason behind this transformation?

- ✓ **Stable Government**
- ✓ **Good Governance**
- ✓ **Better Government Schemes**
- ✓ **Excellent policy**
- ✓ **And public's Developing Mindset**

If we look at the politics of Odisha, the Biju Janata Dal has been in power for more than last 23 years. Development was not particularly visible for the first couple of years after BJD came to power.

I think it took time to build the platform for development. But by then poverty had reached 37% from 47%. However, in the meantime, the government started various schemes in public interest. But those schemes did not prove to be so beneficial for development. But then from 2014 the government launched many developing schemes. And these developing schemes greatly boosted the economy of Odisha.

Today we will discuss only a few major schemes from all those schemes which proved to be the very helpful in the development of Odisha.

- ➢ **Food**
- ➢ **Health Care**
- ➢ **Education**
- ➢ **Housing**
- ➢ **Infrastructure**
- ➢ **Industries**
- ➢ **Agriculture**
- ➢ **Sports**

❖ **<u>Food</u>**:

In some places of Odisha, people used to die without food during 1970-1980. Despite of having all sufficient wealth, people used to die out of hunger in few parts of Odisha at that time. In some districts, people died because of eating mango kernels food in hunger.

The state which shares its 450 km coastline with Bay of Bengal. This state is rich in natural resources and minerals. But if people still died here due to starvation, then what could be more tragic than this?

Poverty and hunger have a very old connection with Odisha. After the Independence, for many decades, Odisha was counted among the poorest states. One of the districts of Odisha is Kalahandi, which was so poor that the country's top VIPs used to come to see it that time. And the names of Indira Gandhi and Rajiv Gandhi are included in these VIPs. Former Prime Ministers used to come to see Kalahandi.

It is said that after seeing Kalahandi's poverty, Indira Gandhi had given a slogan that time *"**Garibi Hatao**"* eliminate the poverty. Which became the most famous and popular slogan of Indira Gandhi at that time. Perhaps due Indira Gandhi's slogan *"Garibi Hatao"*, the poverty of the country reduced but the poverty of Odisha remained the same. There were no changes.

After so much poverty, starvation and bad economic condition, even the natural disasters were not giving up on Odisha. Every year Odisha had to face some or the other natural disasters.

Sometimes cyclone, sometimes drought and sometimes flood. And the biggest example was the super cyclone of 1999. Beginning from wealth to people's lives, how and what types of destruction was happened due to that super cyclone in 1999, that is not hidden from anyone.

The super cyclone had ruined the situation of the entire state almost to such an extent that the then CM Mr. Giridhar Gamang had to resign, situation had become so uncontrolled.

Well, whatever that was all! But after this a new Odisha was born. Which is growing forward and ahead beginning from 2000 to 2023. After the year 2000, Odisha never looked back. The state which was called the poorest state of the country is now known for the country's fastest emerging economy.

The root reason behind this was the assembly Election of 2000. In the year 2000, BJD and BJP together formed the government in the state after the assembly election. But this is not the reason either. The root reason is that Odisha got a new CM Naveen Patnaik. Odisha got a new face, new CM, the youngest son of Biju Patnaik, Naveen Patnaik.

While Naveen took oath as Chief Minister of Odisha in 2000 overfilled with dream, determination and dare. After Naveen Patnaik became the Chief Minister of the state, the new success story that he had started writing for Odisha was clearly visible to the whole world.

His simplicity, his uniqueness, his strong determination and will power, his futuristic thought, his superb planning and great schemes. And among all that great schemes, the most impressive eight schemes are responsible for the success story of Naveen government.

From the eight master stroke, one is food related. If people will not be getting enough food to eat in the state, then how would they think of anything else. If a person's stomach remains empty and he is in hunger, then how would he can think of working further.

In 2000, when Mr. Naveen Patnaik became the CM, there was a major incident in the Kashipur of Raigarh district that hit the headlines. Following the death of 20 people who had consumed gruel made of mango kernels. This negative publicity shook Hon'ble CM Mr. Naveen Patnaik. And that's why the Naveen government decided to give 16 kg of rice per month to every poor at a subsidized rate. This reduced hunger.

Keeping this in mind, both the Central Government and the State Government together started giving rice to the poor people at Rs 2 under central food security scheme. And those who were left out of this scheme, those who were deprived of taking advantage of the scheme, for them, in 2018, the Odisha Government launched its food security scheme and provided rice in Rs 1 per kg to the left out poor families under the state food security scheme.

For this, the state Government had to face an extra financial budget limit of Rs 440 crore. Many people criticized the Government and its policy about this Rs 1 rice. Many people gave many different opinion and said many things regarding this scheme.

But Chief Minister Mr. Naveen Patnaik said it very clearly that;

> *"This is your money, Odisha people's money, I will not let even a single poor person be deprived of food security".*

> *– Mr. Naveen Patnaik*
> *Chief Minister, Odisha*

More than 25 lakh people obliged under this scheme. State Governments own food security scheme proved to be very helpful for those family who really deserved it. Every month, 5 kg rice was given to each member of the family at Rs 1.

Starting from Rs 1 rice to a meal at Rs 5. Mr. Naveen Patnaik used to pay a lot of attention and he ensured that not even a single people of his state should sleep hungry. He believed that it all belongs to the public and they should get its benefits.

That's why he started the meal at just Rs 5. The scheme named *"**Aahar Yojana**"*.

***Aahar Yojana** is a food subsidization program run by the Ministry of Food Supplies and Consumer Welfare, Co-operation, Government of Odisha. The objective is to provide cheap cooked meals to impecunious and needy people. The Government launched it as a pilot project in 5 municipal corporations, Bhubaneswar, Sambalpur, Berhampur, Rourkela and Cuttack and 21 Aahar centers.*

Currently 157 Aahar Centers are active in 30 districts covering 73 towns. Aahar Center are mainly found in places like Hospitals, bus stands, or railway station to serve cooked day meal at just Rs 5. The hygiene of the food is checked by different municipal hospitals. Recently the Government added night meals in 54 Aahar centers near Hospitals to provide needy visitors with cheap and hygiene night meals.

*The **Aahar yojana** was started on April 1st 2015 and inaugurated by CM Naveen Patnaik on Utkal Divas. The actual cost of the food is around Rs 20, but is subsidized to Rs 5 with financial assistance from the Odisha Mining Corporation. It is targeted at more than 60k people per day.*

– Government of Odisha

❖ <u>Health care:</u>

There is very antique saying that *"Swasthya Hee Sampada"*. Health is Wealth. Health is very precious and important for a human being in his life. Well, health related incidents happen in many places all over the world. But because I am from Jagatsinghpur district.

So I will start my chapter with a very painful incident happened in Jagatsinghpur District Medical. A few years ago a man died during his treatment at Jagatsinghpur Medical. And the man's wife could not bear the shock of her husband's death and she committed suicide because of the grief.

This incident shook the entire state.

A healthy society is a sign of a developed society. So that is why it is the primary responsibility of the government to provide affordable health care to all it citizens. Mr. Naveen Patnaik understood this very well. He also had a good sense of awareness regarding health related issues in Odisha.

Mr. Naveen Patnaik knew that how important health is for a healthy society. This is why he is continuing various efforts towards health after coming to power. He has started many health related schemes for public welfare, like Anmol Yojana, Odisha Nidan scheme, Odisha Sahaya scheme, Khushi Yojana, Mamata Yojana and the master piece Biju Swastya Kalyana Yojana.

Mamata Yojana; Under this scheme, the State Government covers the period from the conception of the women till 9 months after the birth of the child, the beneficiary gets Rs 5,000 in four installments.

As a result, there are huge amount of benefits and both mother and child are greatly deprived from health related troubles. The main aim of the Government is to encourage motherhood and provide the mother and child with their health related rights.

To reduce the problem of mother and child's physical inferiority, the Odisha Government has launched this independent scheme Mamata Yojana for pregnant and expecting mothers.

The truth is that after The Almighty God, we are always indebted to a woman. Firstly, for our life and secondly to make us capable of sustaining life. At the root of all life's possibilities, the mother's immense love, service and affection for her child is the root of it. That is why, to overcome the problems of health inferiority the Government of Odisha has made this provision, schemes of Mamata Yojana for the pregnant and expecting mothers.

The health of the child in the womb completely depends on mother's health. If the amount of mother's nutrition decreases during pregnancy, then the fetus inside the womb also gets less amount of nutrition and as a result, low weight children are born.

Various studies have shown that underweight children have very little chance of survival. And those who survive, are affected by various types of diseases and infections and fall ill. There is also a high possibility of becoming a victim of mental illness.

Although Odisha has made progress in reducing maternal and infant deaths. Still the state government has a lot of work to do to achieve the goal. The Naveen Government is extremely serious and concerned about the mother and child health issues. That is why this Mamata Yojana was started in 2011 itself.

In the year 2000 infant mortality rate (the number of deaths per 1000 live births of children under one year of age) was really high, that is, 96 out of 1000 children used to die. Now the number has been reduced to 36 out of 1000.

In Odisha there is 94 first referral units where the emergency cases are handled of new born babies. Along with this 624 Ambulances facility is available 24×7. And which is completely a free service for pregnant women and infant child.

There is 530 new born care center in Odisha and along with that, the children get Vaccines as soon as they are born. And the vaccine is given free with a fine routine. Along with that the child who are more malnourished were sent to Nutritional Rehab center. There is 47 mother and child care complex is available presently, and 19 more care complex is under construction.

In the field of healthcare, "*Nidan*" scheme is also a very important and tremendous initiative of Naveen Government. In this scheme, it provides an advanced healthcare services to the people of Odisha. In this *Nidan* scheme, disease diagnosis and dialysis is available for patient, free of cost in all Government Hospitals, which includes 15 types of important pathology tests, CT Scan, MRI, X-ray, Tele radiology. Lakhs of beneficiaries are benefited through the scheme.

Similarly, another excellent service towards the people of Odisha from Naveen Government is the "*Niramaya Yojana*". This is one of the major healthcare scheme of Odisha Government which was started in the year 2015.

Medicines are providing free of cost in every government hospital and medical colleges from village to city. Keeping in mind the convenience of the patient, the government has taken this decision. People from different groups and the people facing financial problems are benefiting from this facility.

People of any age group can take the benefits of Odisha Niramaya Scheme. The main objective behind launching this scheme is to provide essential medicines to the people of Odisha that to free of cost.

This scheme is also called free Medicine Distribution Scheme of Odisha Government. Under Odisha Niramaya Scheme, Government of Odisha have an aim to provide more than 573 Health related items including essential medicines free of cost to the people of Odisha. At present more than 570 medicines and health related items has been provided.

Few Important Features of Niramaya Scheme;

- ➢ 317 General Items
- ➢ 83 Surgical Items
- ➢ 107 Anti-Cancer Items
- ➢ 21 OSACS
- ➢ 6 Child Health
- ➢ 6 Nutritional Programme.
- ➢ 28 Malaria Control Programme
- ➢ 5 for Leprosy

Not only this, many other important and miraculous works have been done in the field of Health Care by Naveen Government. Which is really commendable. However, there is still a long way to go in the field of Health. And under this effort, many new Medical Colleges and many new hospitals have been opened and few more are under construction and progress in the state.

And the best part is that it can be imagined how sensitive and serious our state Government is regarding Health care that more than Rs 16,000 crores of annual budget is allocated for Health care.

Good health not only has personal importance for a person but is also very important for the entire society and system. Good health determines a better society's foundation. Either it be your own house, your state or your country, a sick man can never imagine a good one. It is important to be healthy for a healthy imagination. And it is the primary right of every common citizen that his government should ensure good, safe and secure facilities for his/her health. Hon'ble Chief Minister Mr. Naveen Patnaik realizes this very well since the early days in politics.

Just imagine if in a middle class family, one member of the family suddenly falls in a serious health issue. What situation will the family members have to face?

Eight lakh rupees is needed for the treatment of that family member who has been hospitalized. That too as soon as possible, it's an emergency situation. And if the operation is not done on time as per the doctor's advice, it can be life threatening. You can imagine the panic situation of that family.

In such a situation, despite all the savings of the family, helps from relatives and all the other efforts, only 3-4 lakhs rupees could be managed. But more 4-5 lakh rupees is required. So what will the head of the family and the family members do in this situation? What is the maximum capacity of a middle class family? There are mourning-like situations at their homes at such times.

In such circumstances, if they go to the bank to take a loan, first of all, the bank will not give them loan so easily. And if the bank gives loan to them then the loan amount along with the interest amount become a huge for them. And by the time they will be able to return back this huge amount to the bank, their condition will be worsened. Would have gone below the poverty line while paying bank EMIs.

So keeping in mind this horrendous health related situation of people. To alleviate such people's suffering, to relieve their suffering. Naveen Government took a historic decision and on 15ᵗʰ August. 2018 The ***Biju Swasthya Kalyan Yojana (BSKY)*** was launched.

The primary health coverage scheme for the welfare of residents of Odisha. Another great and splendid step taken by the BJD Government towards the Healthy Odisha and Happy Odisha resolution. Such a historic, innovative step towards health scheme for the first time in India, it was implemented in Odisha.

Today, lakhs of families and crores of people are taking advantage of this BSKY. Under this BSKY scheme, the Odisha Government will bear all the expenses of getting treated in a government Hospitals. The Naveen Government provides medical assistance of Rs 5 lakh for each family member and an additional Rs 5 lakh for the female member of the beneficiary family, either in Odisha or out of the state this scheme is applicable in the selected private hospitals. This facility has been made available in more than 200 private hospitals across the country.

The people of Odisha will be able to avail this facility within the state or outside the state, and that too in highly modern selected hospitals. Smart Health Cards under Biju Swastya Kalyan Yojana, the state government spends more than Rs 220 crore every month for this scheme only.

How and to what extent this BSKY smart card can be helpful for a helpless family, we will try to know and understand that by true incident. To understand its importance, we will know the grief of a family from Bolangir, Odisha. Under what circumstances could this scheme be helpful to them? This poor family was in complete darkness. The son of the house was suffering from cancer. The whole family was going through a painful storm.

Where will the money come from and how will the cancer operation be done of the man? The family was in a whirlpool of worries.

In such circumstances, a ray of hope was shown in the BSKY smart card. Dhanapati Behera a resident of Phatamunda village, Muribahar block, Bolangir district was suffering from disease like cancer.

In such difficult circumstances the BSKY showed a great hope. Dhanapati was admitted in a private hospital in Visakhapatnam under this scheme. And there he got the successful treatment for his disease. Because of the BSKY smart card, his treatment was provided completely free. The fees which was almost impossible for Dhanapati to pay.

After availing free medical treatment under the state government's scheme, Dhanapati and his family conveyed thanks and blessings to Hon'ble Chief Minister Mr. Naveen Patnaik.

Biju Swastya Kalyan Yojana smart card is now becoming great support and hope for the beneficiaries. Any beneficiary can get the benefit through BSKY smart card even in reputed hospitals like APOLLO, KIIMS, AMRI and TATA Memorial Hospital. Almost all the biggest chain Hospital are included in the list.

Every month Rs 220 crore is spent for the BSKY to provide better healthcare services to the people of Odisha by the Naveen Government. Thousands of medical treatment and surgical procedures are covered under this scheme yet.

Biju Swastya Kalyan Yojana cover the following health care services;

> Free of cost OPD registration.
> Free Medicines.
> Free Diagnostic like Pathology, Radiology, Biochemistry, etc.
> Free Cancer Chemotherapy.
> Free Dialysis Charges.
> Free Operation Theater Charges.
> Free ICU Charges.
> Free IPD Accommodation.
> Free Blood Bank Services
> And more Services are provided under this scheme.

Odisha's Department of Health and family welfare is the Nodal Department of Biju Swastya Kalyan Yojana. The main objective behind launching this scheme is to provide special health protection to the residents of Odisha.

"Biju Swastya Kalyan Yojana" is the flagship scheme of Naveen Government.

❖ <u>**Education**</u>:

"If you want to reach real peace in this world, we should start educating children"

– Mahatma Gandhi

The father of The Nation, Mahatma Gandhi, reminds us the wise thoughts of Bapu on education before starting this chapter which is based on education, its importance and what is the role and responsibility of the Government should be on education.

➢ *True education must correspond to the surrounding circumstances or it is not a healthy growth.*

➢ *What is really needed to make democracy function is not knowledge of facts, but right education*

➢ *You must be the change you wish to see in the world.*

➢ *Live as if you were to die tomorrow, learn as if you were to live forever.*

➢ *Literacy in itself is no education. Literacy is not the end of education or even the beginning. By education, I mean an all-round drawing out of the best in the child and man–body, mind and spirit.*

➢ *Basic education links the children, whether of the cities or the villages, to all that is best and lasting in India.*

➢ *Education should be so revolutionized as to answer the wants of the poorest villager, instead of answering those of an imperial exploiter.*

➢ *The future depends on what we do in the present.*

➢ *There are two days in the year that we cannot do anything, yesterday and tomorrow.*

➢ *If you want to reach real peace in this world, we should start educating children.*

– Mahatma Gandhi

Education is such a basic need, without which, no society, Panchayat, district, state or country can move forward. No country can develop without a good education system. There are many under developed states and countries in this world.

There may be many reasons for this but education is the main reason. Mr. Naveen Patnaik has understood this rhythmically. That is why he has always been more concern and attracted towards education.

He had a very special eye on the education system of Odisha and its transformation. Odisha Government had understood the importance of education. And the government also understood very well that the biggest reason for the un-development of Odisha is education. One of the main reason behind the poverty and backwardness of Odisha was its education system and situation.

So, that's why the Naveen Government is not lagging behind in giving priority to education.

Odisha Government started paying attention to the quality of education along with the school transformations. Along with that, many steps were taken by the state government to increase the literacy rate.

Hon'ble Supreme Court has said that, Education means higher standard of education. But here it was quite the opposite. Forget about high-standard education, even the most important arrangements were not there in the schools. Actually, the education system in Odisha was in a very poor condition a few years ago.

Just imagine if there were no teachers in the school. And the remaining teachers have to protest several times for their basic needs. Sometimes for increase in salary, sometimes for some basic demands for school and sometimes when they did not get their salary on time, they had to go to the capital and stage a protest.

Then how will the teachers concentrate on education? From the office to the teacher's common room, everything was devoid of even the most basic needs. Forget about playground and garden for the students, there was not even a proper toilet at some schools. The classroom was also in the same condition, with broken furniture and no light. In some schools there were few books in a small room in the name of library, that too not in all schools. Students had to face a lot of troubles and poor circumstances.

Those who had money they sent their children to private schools. But poor children kept suffering with these problems. Only a few students could face these problems and continue their study and move ahead in life.

But those who could not do so would leave their study in middle, drop out the school and started searching for some odd work. Leave aside college and higher studies, many students dropped out of school and left home for work, to earn their livelihood outside the state without basic education.

Lack of resources was the reason for poor education. In fact, whenever we used to think about any government schools, a certain kind of picture used to arise in our mind.

A certain type of thought had made a home in our mind about government schools, that government school means there will be all these problems in it. If you want to get more facility, better education than this then you can pay a higher fee in private school and go there.

But now the situation is not like this. Now the situation has changed a lot. Now Odisha has gone a long way in the field of education. There has been a very good change in the field of education. Due to the excellent policies of the Naveen Government, both the condition and direction of the education sector have changed.

This change has become possible due to the visionary thought of the Hon'ble Chief Minister Mr. Naveen Patnaik.

The Naveen Government has created an excellent framework for getting work done. The name of the magnificent structure is 5T. And the Government implemented this splendid structure of 5T not only in education but in other projects also. Through this 5T policy a huge transformation in the education sector has been seen. The profile of high schools across Odisha has changed. The big difference that existed between government schools and private schools has almost disappeared.

Smart classrooms, modern furniture, brighter lighting system, modern and well developed e-library, state-of-the-art laboratory-cum-interactive science centers, advanced sports infrastructure and child friendly campuses, these schools provide an excellent learning experience for students. In the end of third phase more than 6,000 schools have been transformed. All high schools in the state will be covered by the end of the fourth phase.

Overall, the 5T high school transformation program aims to deliver a better learning experience for students in Odisha and to improve their cognitive skills and athletic spirits. The state government has put efforts to develop modern infrastructure and advanced facilities in government schools. Everyone is recognizing the ongoing process of change in the education sector in Odisha with Chief Minister Mr. Naveen Patnaik at the helm.

The Odisha Government is not treating it just as an initiative to streamline the teaching process and develop the infrastructure of the schools, but it is also putting an effort to bring a change in every individual. The endeavor is to bring out the hidden talents in the students and give them an environment that develop their skills, which help them to get the most out of themselves.

"Due to this transformation initiative of our government, enrolment in private schools has come down. Private schools had 16,05,000 students in 2019-20, but the number of students has been reduced to 14,62,000 in 202-22. That

means, 81 percent of students are studying in Government schools". School and Mass Education Minister Mr. Samir Ranjan Dash said.

The 5T school transformation programme has become a model for other states today and has played a vital role in enhancing the interest of the students and parents in the government education institutions.

> *"Education is the most powerful weapon which you can use to change the world"*

> *— Nelson Mandela*

❖ **<u>Housing</u>:**

IMAM ALI (A.S)

"A Beautiful Home Is One Of The Two Paradise".

– Ghurar Al Hikam, Page no- 26

Shelter is a basic human need. Not only humans but from birds to snakes, rats to elephants, everyone needs a home. A home is a place where we feel absolutely safe and secure. A home is a sanctuary where we can retreat from the world and relax. A home provides sense of protection and shelter from the outside world.

Home is a place of emotional attachments with our loved ones. It's a reflection of our identity. Home is an essential aspect of our lives. Our home provides us with a sense of belongingness, comfort, security and stability. It is where we create memories with our loved ones.

The importance of home in our lives cannot be overstated. It is an essential aspect of our well-being and a source of comfort and joy.

You might be wondering why we are talking so much about house? Actually house is not only a necessity in a person's life but it is also a right. Whatever it may be, but everyone should have a home of its own. Whether rich or poor, a home is everyone's basic need.

It is also the responsibility of the government to ensure a shelter for the last man of the society. And we will try to know to what extent the government is successful in providing the same to its people.

Odisha is a state which always competes with natural disasters. From the year 2000 to till date, Odisha has faced cyclone 14 times in continues manner. Every year the people of Odisha have to face this disaster. And in between, sometimes we have to face floods too. In the super cyclone of 1999 only, eighteen thousand houses were completely destroyed.

This trend continues almost every year. Sometimes less and sometimes more damage but it has to face these disasters.

From 1999 super cyclone to Fani cyclone home, farming, shops and all other businesses, people of Odisha have to face loss of crores in many ways. We all witnessed the situation that arose and turned even the capital city Bhubaneswar shattered in Fani cyclone. Many villages were razed to the ground.

In such circumstances, people living in thatched houses had to face a lot of problems. If in storm everything flies away, then in flood everything gets washed away in the flood water. Somewhere, if there is a fear of poisonous snakes entering the house then sometimes there is fear of thieves stealing the house.

People living in thatched houses had to face so many challenges like this. Another biggest problem of people living in thatched houses is that a large part of their earnings every year has to be spent on repairing their house. Due to which other development works of the family gets hampered.

Our legendary leader late Mr. Biju Patnaik, had a dream that *"Every family should have a roof over their head"*.

So, towards fulfilling the dream of Biju Babu, Mr. Naveen Patnaik has done a lot in this direction too. Hon'ble Chief Minister has taken many steps in this direction. Mr. Naveen Patnaik's Government not only provided houses to the beneficiaries but also provided facilities like toilets and money for the repairing of their houses. Under Biju Pakka Ghar Yojana, thousands of beneficiary families have been benefited from this scheme.

To what extent has the Naveen Government provided this facility to beneficiary family? What achievements has BJD Government achieved in this direction? We will know from the Hon'ble Chief Minister Mr. Patnaik himself.

Over to Mr. Chief Minister;

*My dear brothers and sisters, Namaskaar. Home is the identity of a family. A nice house is everyone's dream. There is always a fear of cyclone and floods over Odisha. Nowadays every year we face cyclones. Security of Shelter is the basis of every security. "Every family should have a roof over their head" was Biju Babu's dream. To fulfill this dream we have started **"Biju Pakka Ghar Yojana"**.*

To convert all the Kutcha houses into Pakka houses, our Government has taken decision in the first cabinet of 2014. Very good work has been done in this direction, Odisha is the leading state in the entire country in building houses in rural areas. From 2014 till date, the state government has spent more than Rs 22,000 crores for the housing scheme. To provide a permanent house to the poor people of Odisha, the scheme Biju Pakka Ghar Nirmaan, Shramika Pakka Ghar and Khani Anchala Pakka Ghar has been run from the state government's own treasure.

Along with that, there is Pradhan Mantri Awas Yojana is the central scheme. The state government also bears almost half the expenses for the Central Housing Scheme. Many eligible families have been waiting since a long time to get a house in the central scheme.

But it is very sad that the people of tribal areas and western Odisha, people from such high gravity districts have been specially affected. I have also made the Central Government aware in this regard.

I know many of our poor people are in a lot of trouble due to Covid. Getting minor repair done and even applying white paints in house is becoming difficult for you people. I feel your pain. For this, the state cabinet has taken a historic decision today, to help the poor people we have decided. Your state government is first in the entire country in taking such decisions.

A resolution has been taken in the state cabinet to give a sum of Rs 3,000 for repairing the houses of those who have got houses under Biju Pakka Ghar yojana, Nirman Shramik Pakka Ghar and Khani Anchala Pakka Ghar yojana. Similarly, those families who have been deprived of getting a house in the Central Scheme and are facing troubles, the state government has also taken initiative to provide Rs 5000 assistance for house repair.

Both these assistances will be deposited in the beneficiary's bank account. 30 lakh families will get benefit. This will cost Rs 1444 crores. This expense will be covered through Biju Pakka Ghar Yojana. As long as my government is in power, I will not let the brothers and sisters of my state to suffer for house. I want everyone to live with dignity.

I will try to bring homes from the Central Scheme for you people. But if the Central Government does not accept you people's legal demands. So, you people don't worry. The state Government is with you people. We will take steps in providing you houses.

Jay Jagganath, Bande Utkala Janani
Mr. Naveen Patnaik,
Hon'ble Chief Minister, Odisha

This is the main objective of Biju Pakka Ghar Yojana to build Pakka houses in place of Kacha houses in the rural area of the state. This scheme will definitely play an important role in improving the living standards of the rural and urban areas of poor people. A total of **27,91,452** houses have been built across the state until now. So, this is the achievements and promises for future, of BJD Government's flagship housing programme for the people of Odisha.

"Home sweet home. This is the place to find happiness. If one doesn't find it here, one doesn't find it anywhere".

– M.K. SONI

❖ Infrastructure:

Infrastructure refers to basic systems and services that a state or country needs in order to function properly. The main reason for the development of any state or country is its infrastructure. Infrastructure is categorized into two aspects, one is the Economic Infrastructure and the other is Social Infrastructure.

- **Economic Infrastructure:** It refers to the basic facilities which benefits the process of production and distribution in an economy. For example; Railways, Roads, Ships etc. Availability of power supply accelerate the production activity. In the absence of this it is not possible to develop an efficient system of growth and development.

- **Social Infrastructure:** It refers to elements which helps in human resources development. For example; School, Collage, hospitals and nursing home. It also improves productivity and efficiency. All these come under social Infrastructure.

Infrastructure promotes productivity–

Productivity in primary sector- Agriculture becomes more productive with the permanent means of irrigation.

Productivity in secondary sector- Industrial production depends upon different sources of energy. Like, coal, petroleum, electricity etc. Reduction in the availability of energy may reduce the production and productivity.

Infrastructure induces investments – Infrastructure is the backbone of business investments. Healthy infrastructure facilitates efficient movement of goods and services across different regions of the country.

Infrastructure generates linkages in production – Developed means of transport and communication, ample source of energy along with good facilities of banking and insurance would generate inter-industrial linkages.

Infrastructure enhances size of the market – Means of transport is an important component of economic infrastructure. Efficient transport and communication expands the size of market. Which will increase volume of trade.

Infrastructure enhances ability to work – Social infrastructure enhances the education, skill formation and healthcare which increases the ability to work.

Infrastructure improves quality of life – Lack of hygiene or non-availability of clean drinking water lead to serious health issue. Lack of transport, communication and health infrastructure can make it difficult for people to access healthcare in times of need.

Infrastructure facilities outsourcing – A state or country having a good infrastructure, emerges as a destination for outsourcing. Odisha is emerging to be the destination for call center, study center and medical tourism etc.

So, as we can understand, how the infrastructure of any state or country plays an important role in its development. The entire definition of development lies in the veins of infrastructure. That is why it is said that infrastructure is the backbone of any state. Which creates a network of all the necessary facilities from road communication, rail Communication, sea communication to electricity and airports. Every infrastructure is interconnected and needs each other.

For example, if you need ships and port to export your goods then you also need a truck and road connectivity until port to bring the goods from factory to the ship.

Keeping this in mind, our legendary and visionary leader Biju Babu started this journey many decades ago. Understanding a Port's need and importance he dared to dream and dreamt to build the states only port. As a result, in the year 1962, January the foundation stone of Paradeep Port was laid by the then Prime Minister of India, Late Jawaharlal Nehru. The Port was opened in the year 1966, 12th march.

Not only the Paradeep Port but dozens of such economic infrastructure and social infrastructure are the contributions to Odisha by the legendary hero, late Biju Patnaik, the former Chief Minister. The Orissa Aviation Center, The Cuttack-Jagatpur Mahanadi Highway Bridge, The Bhubaneswar Airport, Express Highway Linking Daitari, Sainik School Bhubaneswar etc. And many more projects are the contributions for Odisha. These were some of the fine achievements of Biju Babu.

Following his father's footsteps, fulfilling his father's dream and taking them further Mr. Naveen Patnaik have done a splendid job. By balancing every area for the development of Odisha. From education to healthcare and agriculture to transport. Today Odisha is changing faster. There has been a lot of change in infrastructure in Odisha in the last few years, which has changed the outlook of the entire state. Development work is going on rapidly in every sector.

Along with this, road connectivity work is also being done in a tremendous manner to connect the village with the city. Particularly remote areas are being connecting with major cities. Development of villages along with the city is also going on in parallel manner.

Mr. Naveen Patnaik himself and his government understood every category and aspects of infrastructure very well. In every aspect of infrastructure, the Naveen government is doing tremendous job with great sharpness. Be it the Economic Infrastructure or Social Infrastructure. The government is working at great pace on both the aspects of infrastructure.

If we talk about social infrastructure, then the Naveen government is implementing the entire strategy by considering the complete situation of present and future development of the state. Equal progress is being going on at every branch that comes under social infrastructure.

Where on one side you will see that almost all the high schools of Odisha are being transformed. Beautification and development work with all modern facilities is being done under the government's 5T plan then on the other hand, you will also see that almost every police station in the state are shining like same and also being upgraded with a friendly environment.

Transformation of every police station of the state is being done with friendly environment. So that people should not feel hesitation or fear to go to any police station and feel themselves comfortable. The government makes sure, the common citizen should feel that the police and the police station is to serve them, to serve a common man.

In the same way, nowadays if you go to any government hospital then it will be very difficult for you to judge whether you are standing in a government hospital or a private nursing home. Because under the Naveen government's splendid 5T plan, the transformation of government hospitals in the entire state has also been done in an excellent manner.

The government hospital also looks like a wonderful hi-tech modern private hospital in the state, which is fully equipped with modern facilities. Not only this, all the fire stations in the state have also been upgraded.

We are talking about the development of social infrastructure of Odisha. this discussion cannot be completed without remembering the SCBMCH. Srirama Chandra Bhanja Medical Collage and Hospital, famously known as SCB Medical, Cuttack. Which was established in the year 1944 on 1st June.

One of the oldest centers of medical teaching and training in India, located in the heart of the city Cuttack with a sprawling campus of

101 acres. The redeveloping work of this premier medical college is going on, on its full pace. The SCB Mega Development Plan is one of his dream project of The Hon'ble Chief Minister Mr. Naveen Patnaik to convert into a world-class health institution.

Another chapter has been added to the history of development of Odisha. With an estimated cost of Rs 3,500 crores, a state-of-the-art 5,000 beds integrated hospital, equipped with latest medical equipment and facilities and developed on an area of 175 acres. Under this transformational initiative, 1,280 staff quarters, additional hostel facilities for 2,000 more students, modern restaurants, commercial centers, facilities for recreation and sports with adequate security provisions included in this mega AIIMS plus category institution.

"It is my dream that all people of Odisha have access to high quality and affordable healthcare. A good many Odia doctors serving outside the state and abroad have earned name and fame for their outstanding service in healthcare. We are trying to create a better environment to give these doctors an opportunity to serve their motherland".

"The SCB Medical College and Hospital has been serving the people of Odisha since 1944. It has produced brilliant doctors who have served and continue to serve patients not only in Odisha but across the globe. They are the pride of our state. It is now upon us to transform this great institution into a world-class facility". The Hon'ble Chief Minister Mr. Naveen Patnaik said.

Not only the SCB Medical College and Hospital's transformation and redevelopment is going on but almost all the social infrastructure's aspects are under the super vision of our splendid visionary leader, Chief Minister Mr. Naveen Patnaik's action plan 5T.

All the government high schools, government hospitals, police stations, fire stations or any other social infrastructure etc. Everywhere Development work is going on rapidly in every sector. Some projects have been completed, some are in progress and others are being planned. So, this was few glimpses of social infrastructure development story of Naveen government.

Now let's move towards the Economic Infrastructure Development of Odisha. If we will talk about the economic infrastructure of the state, then here also the BJD government raising the flag of development. Odisha has several mining-based industrial houses, which offers long-term potential for cargo handling by Odisha's leveraging 480 km coastline. While the state at present has three all-weather ports at Paradeep, Dhamra and Gopalpur. Three more ports at Astaranga, Subarnarekha Mouth and a riverine port near Mahakalapada are expected to be ready in a few years. The state government has also identified nine more port locations. The BJD government has always given importance to the development of infrastructure projects like roads, railway, airports and ports.

To carry out all these development works faster, smoothly and in proper manner in the state, an organization has been established. Odisha Industrial Infrastructure Development Corporation (IDCO) was set up by the Government of Odisha as a statutory Corporation in 1981. IDCO has been acting as the Nodal Agency for providing industrial infrastructure and land for industrial and infrastructure projects in the state. The objective of the corporation is to provide infrastructure services for rapid establishment and orderly growth of industry, trade and commerce in Odisha.

This is the reason why an organization like IDCO was established in the year 1981. Few Infrastructure Projects are discussed briefly;

> **Special Economic Zone (SEZ):** Two SEZs have been developed by IDCO. Info city SEZ of IDCO at Chandaka (Bhubaneswar) developed over an area of 145.91 acre is in operation. Mind

Tree, TCS, WIPRO have established their unit in this SEZ. A sector Specific IT/ITES SEZ is under implementation at Gaudakasipur near Bhubaneswar (Info Valley) over the area of 262 acres of land. M/s Infosys is the anchor tenant for this SEZ which has been allotted Ac. 50.909 of land in the park.

> **Electronic Manufacturing Cluster (EMC):** IDCO is developing an electronic hardware manufacturing cluster at Info valley under the Electronics Manufacturing Cluster Scheme of Ministry of Electronics & Information Technology (MeitY), Government of India.

> **Petroleum, Chemical Petrochemical Investment Region (PCPIR):** Under the PCPIR Scheme of Govt. of India, the state govt. is developing a PCPIR at Paradeep to be set up on 284.15 sq km (70,214 acres) of land spread over Jagatsinghpur and Kendrapara districts. The PCPIR hub is expected to attract investment to the tune of Rs 2.74 lakh crore. Indian oil Corporation Ltd (IOCL) is the anchor tenant for the project. Around 3,300 acres of land have been acquired and handed over to IOCL for its 15 million tons per annum oil refinery with an investment of approximately Rs30,000 crores.

IOCL has also announced implementation of 700 KT per Annum Polypropylene unit at Paradeep with an investment of Rs 3,150 crores. IDCO has formed an SPV, Paradeep Investment Region Development Ltd for development required infrastructure for the project, IDCO has undertaken land of approximately 7400 Acres for industrial development in the PCPIR. The state government, meanwhile, is in the process of identifying new anchor tenants interested in setting up petrochemical cracker units within the PCPIR region.

> **Special Investment Region (SIR):** Basedon the development of Dhamra Port and upcoming LNG terminal facility by IOCL

at Dhamra. Government is contemplating to develop a Special Investment Region spread over 10,000 acres of land in 43 villages and notified it as lease barred area. A Special Act has also been prepared. The SIR shall have delineated zone for industrial, social, logistic, residential etc. It shall create opportunity for manufacturing industries in the sector of downstream in Aluminum and Steel, fertilizer and other Gas based industries and Wood based industries etc.

➢ **Kalinga Nagar National Investment Manufacturing Zone:** The Steel Complex at Kalinga Nagar established over an area of 13,000 acres of land where 9 major Steel Companies has already set-up their units and are producing 3.5 Million tonnes of steel per annum and has generated 40,000 employments.

➢ **Plastic Park at Paradeep:** To promote industries in plastic and polymer sector, a Plastic Park over 120 acres of land is being development in PCPIR at refinery Complex of IOCL.

➢ **Seafood Park, Deras:** IDCO is developing a Seafood park at Deras over an area of 152.78 acres of land. The project is developed under the Mega Food Parks Scheme of Ministry of Food Processing Industries (MoFPI), Government of India. The total project cost as approved by the MoFPI, Government of India is Rs 125.42 Crore.

➢ **Aluminum Park:** For Promotion of investment in downstream & ancillary units in the Aluminum sector, Angul Aluminum Park is being developed jointly by IDCO and NALCO over 223 acres of land at Angul.

➢ **Convention**-cum- Trade Zone Center: IDCO on behalf of the government is developing a Convention cum Trade Zone (CTZ) at Janata Maidan in Bhubaneswar.

➢ **Agro Industrial Estate:** Department of Agriculture and Farmers Empowerment, Government of Odisha is establishing an Agro Industrial Estate in semela village under Papadahandi block of Nawarangapur district through IDCO with a project cost of Rs 12.76 crore. The industrial Estate is implemented over an area of 69.81 acres of land.

- ➢ **Tower-2010 at Mancheswar:** In order to provide built-up space for promotion of IT/ITES industries in the state, IDCO has taken up construction of a G + 17 storied with 4.52 lakh sft. Super built up area. The cost of the project is Rs 140 crores.

- ➢ **Construction of IT Incubation Center:** An It Incubation center is being developed in the Infocity IT/ITES SEZ, Chandaka, Bhubaneswar. Over an area of 2.39 acres of land with a built up area 33.048 sqm. This complex will have two towers with a 200 seated IT Incubator, built up space for IT/ITES companies, a commercial complex and other amenities.

- ➢ **Construction of Office-cum-Commercial Complex in different districts:** IDCO has taken initiative to construct office-cum-Commercial Complexes in different district of the state to attract Corporate Houses to open up their business activities there.

- ➢ **Development of National Waterways (NW)-5:** For development an Inland Navigation System for movement of cargo from the industries and mines to the ports, a MoU has been signed between Government of Odisha, Inland Waterways Authority of India (IWAI), Paradeep Port Trust and Dhamra port for the stretch between Talcher to Paradeep and Dhamra to National Waterways (NW)-5.

- ➢ **Textile Park at Dhamnagar:** IDCO has contemplated to establish a Textile Park over 234 acres of land available near Dhamnagar in Bhadrak district.

It's worth noting that these are just a few examples and there are many more policies, efforts and achievements of BJD government and its supremo Mr. Naveen Patnaik.

According to an ANI report published in The Economic Times. The Odisha government approved nine industrial projects worth Rs 873.57 crores which will create employments opportunity for 2,51600 people in the state.

Odisha Government's State Level Single Window Clearance authority (SLSWCA) has approved nine industrial projects. The projects include;

➤ Petronet LNG Limited's Compressed Bio Gas and Fermented Organic Manure Plant. With an annual capacity of 33,065 MT, this project promises a dual advantage of chemical production and renewal energy, said officials. Located in Deogarh, this initiative is set to transform the landscape, the official added.

➤ Pearl Precision Products Pvt Ltd joins the ranks with their plan for a cutting-edge Plastic Faucet, Water Tank, Pipes and Fitting manufacturing unit. This project will be coming up in Paradeep Plastic Park, Jagatsinghpur.

➤ In the plastic sector, Indopet Polyplast Pvt. Ltd. sets out to establish a high capacity manufacturing unit for Food Grade Pet Bottles, Jars and Pre-Forms, with an annual capacity of 8,000 MT. strategically located in Khurda, this projects stands to enhance both employment opportunity and plastic manufacturing excellence.

➤ The steel industry's ancillary sector gathers momentum with the approval of TRL Krosaki Refractories Ltd.'s comprehensive project. Spanning 57,000 MT basic raw material grinding unit, 11,700 MT monolithic raw material grinding unit, 8,900 MT high alumina raw material grinding unit and 14,400 MT grog processing unit, this venture is located in Jharsuguda.

➤ Another project is Chosun Sarvesh Refractories Private Limited's 14,400 MT Tap Hole Clay unit. It will be located at Kuanramunda, Sundergarh. Chosun is a South Korean Company with having reputable stature as a manufacturer of quality refractories.

➢ Saizar Enterprise Private limited enriches the steel (Downstream) domain by erecting a Steel processing unit for HR & CR coil. Situated in Kalinga Nagar, Jajpur, this project will add to Odisha's steel processing capacity.

➢ Vikram Private Limited's expansion project for a 0.12 MTPA SMS and 0.1 MTPA TMT plant adds yet another dimension to Odisha's steel manufacturing prowess. Located in Lahunipada, Sundergarh, this initiative is another addition to Odisha's strong steel sector.

➢ The Agro and Food Processing sector receives a substantial boost with Coastal Biotech Private Limited's Corn Processing and corn starch manufacturing unit. This venture, situated in Bamuni Industrial Estate in Nawarangapur district will leverage the district's maize production capacity.

➢ Odisha's tourism Landscape thrives with the ambitious project of SNM Hotel and Resorts private limited. The Hotel and Resort facility will be coming up in chikiti, Ganjam. The project in the tourism sector underpins the state's efforts for broad-based industrial growth, said official. (ANI).

So, these were some glimpses of the wonderful journey of the Naveen Government. Some important decisions, some great plans and steps taken towards the development of the state, Odisha. Which is clearly visible not only in the state but in the entire country. That's how Odisha has been on the path of progress during the last two decades. Everyday Odisha is writing a new chapter of success.

Every area that was left behind over the decades, the Naveen Government is working on it with great precision and justice. This Government is working keeping in mind the progress of every section of the society.

Even if it is about electricity reaching the house of the last person of the state, be it a bus stand, a railway station or the states only international airport. State government has its sharp and first eyes on the progress of every sector.

According to a report till 2011-12, there was electricity only in the 60% of the houses in the state. Which means 40% of family in the state were deprived from the electricity. But once in the Lok Sabha, while replying to the question of MP Chandrani Murmu, Union Power Minister had said that the Odisha Government had claimed that almost 100% villages had been electrified by April 18,2018.

Cuttack, the oldest city of Odisha, whose history is more than of 1000 years. But this historic city of Odisha is still longing for many basic facilities. But after coming to power, the Naveen Government is making every effort to change its condition and direction. Whether we talk about the transformation and redevelopment of SCB Medical and Hospital or the same effort for Badambadi bus stand, the oldest bus stands of the city.

Now It is being a wonderful experience for the travelers who come from every corner of Odisha to Cuttack. Because now the Badambadi bus stand is turning into a modern class G + 2 bus terminal named after Netaji Subhas Chandra Bose Bus Terminal in Cuttack's Khan Nagar. The Government has provided facilities like railway stations and airports at one place. This modern bus stand terminal has a total of 33 rooms. More than 200 buses can park simultaneously in this bus terminal at a time.

There are separate routes for the exit and entry of buses. Restrooms are also available for drivers in this bus terminal building. There is dormitory for female and male passengers. It also has an Information Center for the convenience of passengers for getting bus details and other general information etc. and if we will talk about security then there is a 24x7 CCTV cameras along with a police outpost.

We not only hope but are sure that this Hi-Tech Modern Bus terminal will bring great happiness and comfort to the travelers coming to Cuttack.

Similarly, the Baramunda bus stand of Bhubaneswar is also being transformed into Odisha's first world class transit system. All the modern facilities are available in this bus terminal. More than 2000 buses will travel to and from this bus terminal.

Built at a cost of Rs 180 crore, this bus terminal is spread over 11 acres of land. Which is equipped with many modern facilities like, Elevator, Escalator, Food Court, Shop, Wi-Fi, Aahar Center, Information Center etc. Facility to pick-up and drop passengers is also available here. One of the most important thing is that the entire terminal is operating through solar power energy.

Odisha is well known for its rich cultural heritage, historical landmark and breathtaking landscapes. The eastern state has witnessed significant developments in its aviation infrastructure too in recent years under the rule of the visionary Chief Minister Mr. Naveen Patnaik.

The state has seen the establishment of several airports, from domestic to international terminals. And these airports serve as crucial gateways to the region, offering convenient access to both domestic and international destinations. Odisha provides tourist from all over the world with the variety of site seeing options, from beaches to religious monuments. The airports play a pivotal role in promoting tourism, trade and cultural exchange, contributing to the state's economic and cultural diversity.

Like every other sector, the BJD Government is doing great work in Aviation too. As a result, Odisha is converting to home to several domestic airports that enhance regional air travel gradually. These airports serve as vital transportation hubs, connecting the state's diverse landscapes and cultures. They facilitate and convenient to access various cities within India, promoting tourism, trade, and interconnectivity within the country.

These domestic airports play a significant role in advancing economic growth and fostering regional development in Odisha. And Odisha is moving towards a bright and golden future.

❖ <u>**Industries**</u>:

Industrialization is not a sudden change but a gradual change that happens over a period. Industrialization is defined as the process or period of social and economic growth and transformation of an agricultural society to an industrial society. In simple words, Industrialization is the process of changing an agriculture-based economy to an economy based on manufacturing goods. In the process, many changes take place that helps the economy of the society grow and prosper.

A few years ago, Odisha was an Agriculture based economy. Although agriculture is a huge strength for any state and any country. But agriculture based economy is never being a stable economy. Especially in a state like Odisha where natural disasters are so common. Odisha is cyclone prone state. Almost every year Odisha has to face any natural disaster. Mr. Naveen Patnaik had understood this factor very well after coming to power in the year 2000. That's why right after coming to power, Mr. Patnaik gradually started changing the economic policy of Odisha. The best part is that he very soon succeeded in his objective to a great extent. And very soon, along with promoting agriculture, he also adopted industrialization in Odisha to lay a strong and durable economy in the state.

As a result, according to an economic survey of 2022-23, Odisha's 41.03% of GSDP is coming from industry sector only. Which was only 26% GSDP was coming in the year 2011. GSDP means, Gross State Domestic Product. For example, the economic activity of all goods and services at the All India Level is called GDP. Similarly, all the goods and services economic activities within the state are referred to GSDP.

Odisha is endowed with vast resources of a variety of minerals and occupies a prominent place in the country as a mineral rich state. Abundant reserves of high-grade Iron ore, Bauxite, Chromite, Manganese, ore along with other minerals such as coal, limestone, Dolomite, Tin, Nickel,

Vanadium, Lead, Graphite, Gold, Gemstone, Diamond, Dimension & Decorative stone etc.

This has opened up Immense possibilities for locating mineral based industries for manufacturing of Steel, Ferro-alloys, Cement, Alumina/Aluminum, Refractories, Thermal power etc. Odisha has about 28 percent of India's iron ore, 24 percent of coal, 59 percent of bauxite and 98 percent Chromite. Odisha is an ideal location for setting up aluminum and aluminum- based companies because of its 55 percent of bauxite reserves.

Not only this, but now Odisha is one of the favored investment destinations for domestic and international iron and steel players as well as one of the largest producers of iron and steel in India. Odisha has sector-specific policies for IT and micro, small and medium enterprises. The state government has constituted "Team Odisha" to help with investment promotion. As a result, Odisha is amongst the top ten states accounting for the highest number of MSME enterprises.

The state's BJD government also launched its startup policy 2016. The policy aims to provide incentives, support and assistance to start ups at all stages of development including idea or prototype stage, commercialization stage as well as the marketing stage.

The Odisha Industry is going places with excellent industrial infrastructure and presence of top national and international companies. The state has witnessed an industrial upsurge due to the favorable industrial atmosphere in the state. The Naveen Government has invited major industrial houses of the country and abroad to invest in the state. It had achieved an excellent considerable amount of success and several prime companies have set up their plants in the state.

All these development is not just happened over night. This is the result of the great visionary leader's futuristic plan, strong determination, deep love and passion for his state and its people. Indeed, this is the result of our Hon'ble Chief Minister's Mr. Naveen Patnaik's Good Governing. Few major initiatives taken by the BJD Government to promote Odisha as an investment destination:

➤ The BJD Government unveiled a strategic action plan for the implementation of the "Vision 2025" which lays a road map for industrial growth in the state over the next decade. The state government has identified five focus sectors that include agro and food processing, chemicals and petrochemicals, textiles and apparel, downstream and ancillary industries in metal sector and electronic system design and manufacturing and IT/ITES. The plan covers, policy, infrastructure, investment promotion and skilling interventions that the state government plans to undertake for industrial development in these focus sectors.

➤ The state Government also launched an advanced version of its industrial portal for land use and services i.e GOiPLUS. The GOiPLUS Version 2.0 provides information about the entire land bank available in the state for industrial use and works as a one-stop portal to provide information about all land related queries of an investor. Using the portal, an investor can get information about availability of land parcel in the vicinity of preferred infrastructure utilities such as airports, port etc.

➤ In order to increase the employment opportunity in the state, Odisha government has announced plans to invest US$ 28.69 billion in the manufacturing sector generating nearly three lakh job opportunities.

➤ In June 2015, in an effort to increase the traffic of foreign airlines in the state, the state government exempted the Value Added Tax (VAT) imposed on aviation turbine fuel.

➤ In July 2015, the state government announced plans to frame a rural Business Process Outsourcing (BPO) scheme under which subsidies are planned to be offered for establishing BPO units. In places where STPI (Software Technology Parks of India) stations are situated, employment opportunities are expected to be generated in the state. STPIs in the state are located in Bhubaneswar, Balasore, Rourkela and Berhampur.

➢ As per budget 2016-17, US$ 39.71 million has been proposed by the state government for developing new railway projects such as the ongoing Khurda-Bolangirline, new Jaypore-Malkangiri, Jaypore-Nabarangapur railway lines, etc. in the state through direct state funding.

➢ As per state budget 2016-17, the state government allocated US$ 1.52 million for development and enhancement of eco-tourism in Odisha.

➢ A biopharma IT park at Bhubaneswar is being established under the public private partnership (PPP) model over a land area of 64.68 acres.

➢ A mega food park is being established near Bhubaneswar over 282 acres through the PPP mode. Odisha Industrial Development Corporation (IDCO) is the nodal agency for the establishment of this park.

➢ In order to strengthen the artisan-based enterprises in the handicrafts sector, 19 handicraft training centers are functioning in different districts. **Courtesy- OPSC Notes.**

Odisha's annual industrial growth rate better than the national average: NABARD

The annual average growth rate of the industry sector in the costal State during the last 10 years is projected at 5.36% as against 3.77% at the national level, according to the State Focus Paper (2022-23) study conducted by National Bank for Agriculture and Rural Development (NABARD).

The industry sector continues to have a growing contribution in the state's Gross Value Added (GVA) economic productivity metric, with a 36.26% share to 26% at the National Level.

Odisha's industry sector has contracted by 8.83% in comparison to the 9.57% contraction rate at the national level in 2020-21.

The manufacturing sector is the largest contributor with a share of over 48.4% in 2020-21, followed by the mining sector (24.60%). The state government has taken numerous measures like Make in Odisha and reforms under "Ease of Doing Business" accomplish steady and fast industrialization in large, medium and small industries, the reports said.

In the steel sector, the state stands as the largest steel and stainless steel producer in the country. The state has 2 large Public Sector Undertakings (PSUs)- Rourkela Steel Plant & Neelachal Ispat Nigam. Also, Odisha is the highest producer of Aluminium in the country today with two of the largest Aluminium Plants viz., Nalco and Vedanta Limited.

The service sector continues to be the leading broad sector in the state's economy and as per advance estimate; it is expected to contribute about 42.47% of Odisha's GVA in 2020-21.

Trade, repair, hotels and restaurants sub-sectors are expected to account for about 22% share of output from services, followed by transport and communication. With the increasing stress on providing banking services to the unbanked population, the financial services sector may get a boost.

An extensive and reliable infrastructure network is the prime requirements for sustainable economic growth. It not only facilitates functioning of the economy and social sectors, but also accelerates economic growth with better competitiveness, the NABARD study suggested.

Odisha, has immense scope for improving the extent and quality of its infrastructure facilities. The socio-economic development is the key to overall growth of the economy. Besides agricultural infrastructure, there also exists immense scope for creation of other infrastructure in areas like housing, food and safe drinking water and social needs like education, health care and domestic energy. Such interventions are always crucial to enhance the standard of living of the people, the NABARD's State Focus Paper pointed out. **Courtesy; The Statesman**

"Odisha is one of the fastest growing economies in India and has consistently grown above the national average in the last decade and a half. We are fast emerging as a major industrial destination in eastern India because of our natural resources advantage and strategic location.

Over the last 20 years, my government has focused on leveraging these natural advantages through progressive policy, efficient administration, and technological interventions". Hon'ble Chief Minister Mr. Naveen Patnaik was speaking at the curtain raiser for Make in Odisha Conclave'22.

❖ <u>Agriculture</u>:

Agriculture is the world's oldest profession is the main source of life sustenance for the human population. Agriculture is defined as the process of crops cultivation and the raising of livestock animals for producing food, feed, fiber and other desired products. The agriculture sector continues to be the mainstay of livelihood for human civilization. The Agricultural growth is important not only for ensuring food security and reduction of poverty in rural areas but also for sustainable growth of the rest of the economy.

In Odisha, the agriculture sector is the major contributor to the state's economy. Approximately 76% of the total working population in Odisha is engaged with the agriculture sector. Odisha employees about 73% of it and its population in farming contributes around 30% to the Net State Domestic Product as an agrarian economy. Around 40% that is roughly around 87.46 lakh hectares' area are brought to the agriculture sector every year.

The major crops cultivated in Odisha are Rice, Pulses, Oil Seeds, Jute, Coconut and Turmeric, Tea, Cotton, Groundnut and rubber crops are of great economic importance in other parts of Odisha. Odisha mainly contributes one-tenth of the total rice produced in the country. Some other important food grains are oilseeds (groundnut, mustard, castor oil) and pulses (gram, tur and arhar).

Various cash crops are also cultivated in Odisha. Some of the important cash crops in Odisha include Jute, Mesta, Sugarcane, Tobacco, Rubber, Tea, Coffee and Turmeric. These crops are cultivated across different geographical areas of the state.

Odisha is one of the largest producers of rice. Agriculture and farmers are the backbone of a country's development. 73% people in Odisha depend on agriculture. And with one year's hard work of the 73% people, it is being possible to provide food to all the people of the state. But whenever it comes to Farming and Farmers. At that time, many voices and problems also come under the discussions and debate. Till about the 90s, the agriculture sector used to be managed in the traditional style in Odisha. but at the very beginning of the 21st century, the development of basic skills and technology in farming had created a lot of potential and hope in the agriculture sector.

Meanwhile, many political parties came to power in Odisha by promising to solve the problems of farming and farmers in the state. But the farmers of Odisha did not get much benefit from the promises, they faced a great deal of disappointment. Sometimes, due to excessive rains, the farmers had to face floods and due to flood the entire crop was ruined.

And sometimes farmers have to face drought due to no rain. And many times even the farmers' suicides make headlines in several places. Which was very horrendous, painful and disappointing? Due to such condition of farmers, many times the state had to face food shortage. It is not only ends with the food shortage in the state but in many places of Odisha people had died due to starvation.

Although, the condition of Odisha was almost the same everywhere, but we would like to remind the past of Kalahandi. Kalahandi, is the name of one of the thirty districts of Odisha. Whose name only used to bring a different lower feeling in the hearts and mind of people on hearing its name. Backward place, poverty, starvation, child selling, some such very painful words were used to heard about this place then. In the year 1866, which provided food to the severe famine Banga Pradesh. That place was being ridiculed.

All of India felt agitated when the heart-touching tale of Phanas Punji made it into national television. The tale of Phanas Punji not only shocked the nation but also had shocked the world in 1985. Phanas Punji of Amalapalli village in Kalahandi, Odisha, had sold her tow-year-old sister-in-law for Rs 40 to save her own two starving littles ones. Punjis tale, as highlighted by INDIA TODAY in dated July 31, 1985. The tale of such acute destitution spread like wildfire, and soon Phanas Punji got personified as Odisha's poverty. The then Prime Minister Rajiv Gandhi flew to Odisha to meet Phanas Punji.

"Here children are sold cheaper than *channas* (legumes)"! Says Kapil Narain Tiwari, a former MLA.

So, this was the saddened tale of not only Kalahandi but almost the state. But it is said that every dark night has a golden morning. Starvation, Poverty, Drought, Flood and Farmer Suicide case. Many such heart-wrenching words were used to heard in Odisha in those days.

But today Chief Minister Mr. Naveen Patnaik proudly say that; *"Kalahandi is no longer the land of hunger and has been transformed into Odisha's rice bowl"*. Said Hon'ble Chief Minister Naveen Patnaik.

Today Odisha is exporting rice. How…?

As it is said that every dark night has a golden morning. So, Odisha also started seeing its golden rays of morning while Mr. Naveen Patnaik took oath as the Chief Minister of Odisha in the year 2000.

The day and decades started changing and everything started changing with it. Indravati broke her silence. And the waves of Indravati started singing about the shining and golden future of Kalahandi. Why only Kalahandi but the entire Odisha started seeing this golden bright future of farmers and agriculture sector.

The fort of success on which Odisha and its farmers stand today, planting of its seeds was done two decades ago. With the development of knowledge and skills, new possibilities were created for the agriculture sector.

Anyone feels elated after seeing the lush green crops and the waving crops growing in the ground. But do you know how much hard work is involved in growing this golden crop of a farmer? Do we ever realize what conditions and circumstances each farmer has to go through to bring the grains into our plate?

Odisha lives in its village and farmers are its backbone. In Odisha 64.09 lakh hectares' land is useful for agriculture. Out of which almost 60.50 lakh hectares of land is currently cultivating. And the fate of 70% people of Odisha is linked with this cultivation.

When the Naveen government came into power. Farmers used to get government support on the basis of agriculture policy prevalent in 1996. Which was like one bowl of water to the ocean. The supports from the government to the farmers were not enough in any angle. That's why in the second term of his rule in 2008, Naveen government introduced new policy in agriculture. But yet Mr. Chief Minister didn't let divert his focus from farming and farmers. In the third phase of his rule in 2013, going one step further, Naveen government brings again new policies in the agriculture sector.

The BJD government has always prioritized the interests of the farmers and those engaged in farming activities, including the landless agricultural workers. Several innovative schemes have been initiated for our farmers and to increase farm productivity, which have resulted in agricultural production increase over the last two decades. Besides, the state government presented a separate agricultural budget for the first time. Many schemes have been initiated for all types farming, for the bright, safe and secure future of farmers. The Naveen Government have been very particular and focused in all aspects of agriculture sector.

- ➤ Kalia Yojana (December 2018)
- ➤ Mukhyamantri Krishi Udyog Yojana (May 2018)
- ➤ Mukhyamantri Abhinav Krishi Yantripati Samman Yojana (May 2018)

> Bhoochetana (April 2018)
> Odisha Free Smartphone Yojana for women Farmers (April 2018)
> Mobile for Farmers (December 2017)
> Odisha Fish Pond Yojana (November 2017)
> Mukhyamantri Adibandha Yojana (March 2017)
> Biju Krushak Kalyan Yojana (2013)
> Matsyajibi Basagruha Yojana (2014)
> Matsyajibi Unnayana Yojana (2003)

Above is the list of few major schemes ran by the government of Odisha. The Biju Janta Dal Government initiated various schemes from time to time for the welfare of farmers and for the development of agriculture sector in the state.

KALIA: Krushak Assistance for Livelihood and Income Augmentation (KALIA) is the flagship Scheme of Naveen Government for the farmers of Odisha. The government of Odisha launched the Kalia Yojana to reduce poverty and accelerate agricultural prosperity. It is a scheme that provides various benefits for farmer's welfare. The KALIA Scheme supports cultivators, small farmers and landless agricultural labourers. It provides payment to farmers to encourage cultivation and associated activities.

The plan is expected to benefit over 30 lakh smallholder farmers in the state. A sum of Rupees. 10,000 crores will be allocated each year for the Rabi Season and Rabi Crops, with 5,000 crores allocated for all these seasons. These handouts are given to assist people to buy seeds and fertilizers for their gardens.

The Naveen government's main aims and objective for introducing this plan is as bellow:

• The government's first and greatest goal is to free debt-ridden farmers from their debt burden, and more than Rs. 10,000 crores have been set aside for this purpose.

- Directly combat poverty by giving financial aid to the state's most disadvantaged farm households, landless laborers and marginal growers.
- To assist 92% of the state's growers and nearly all landless cultivators.
- To offer farmers with an accessible and adoptive support system.
- Agriculture sector development.
- Ensure that agricultural productivity is maintained.
- Farmers' income should be increased.

Kalia Yojana Scheme Benefit: Odisha government runs the Krushak Assistance for Livelihood and Income Augmentation Program. This scheme was introduced by the government of Odisha for farmers, cultivators, croppers and landless agriculture labourers. The government will give the following advantages to the scheme's participants under this scheme:

- The first and most important benefit of this framework is that the government will provide financial assistance to small-scale farmers by providing Rs 25,000 per household over five years to assist them purchase inputs such as seeds fertilizers and pesticides, as well as use assistance for labour and other investments.
- Every impoverished Agricultural Household would get Rs. 12,500 for agricultural linked activities such as small goat raising units, mini-layer units, duckery units, fisheries kits for fisherman, mushroom farming and bee-keeping and so on.
- Vulnerable farmers and landless agricultural labourers would get Rs. 10,000 per household per year to assist them survive.
- The beneficiaries have access to a Rs. 2 lakh life insurance policy with a Rs. 330 premium payments.
- All beneficiaries will also receive a Rs. 2 lakhs accidental coverage at a premium of Rs. 2.
- Farmers will also be provided with a crop loan of Rs. 50,000 at 0% interest.

According to the Activity Report 2019-20. Department of Agriculture and Farmer's Empowerment. Government of Odisha:

A plethora of development interventions have led to an increase in production and productivity of different crops. The food grain production was 85 lakh MT during 2017-18 inspite of moisture stress conditions and pest epidemic inflicting a colossal crop loss and estimated at 97 lakh MT during 2018-19 as per final estimates even after the unfavourable impact of Titli-Cyclone. Similarly, 2019-20, the advance estimates reveal a much better production of 118 lakh MT although the state suffered crop loss on account of FANNI and BulBul during Kharif 2019.

Inspite of all these, not only has the state become self-sufficient but also surplus in food grains. More so, the state has been conferred with Krishi Karman Award (Commendation Award) for the fifth time during 2019-20 for its performance in food grain production sector during 2016-17 adding a feather to its cap.

The productivity of rice has doubled and food grain production has gone up substantially inspite of extreme weather events visiting the state almost every year. There is an ambitious program to produce around 124 lakh MT of food grains during 2020-21.

Massive efforts are being made for incentivizing cultivation of non-paddy crops i.e. pulses, oilseeds, and cotton and horticulture crops under state plan. This is expected to help in diversion of crop land to more remunerative crops reducing the greater bias towards paddy.

Around 2 lakh demonstrations and more than 5200 farmer's training, involving 4.5 lakh farmers, on various production technologies in different crops have been conducted with the objective of transferring the cutting edge technologies in crop production and post-harvest management of agri-produces.

Increased environmental concerns have put Soil Health Management high on state's developmental agenda. Besides, sustainable crop production strategies have rendered up-keeping soil health with greater importance in modern crop husbandry. There are 30 static and 17 mobile soil testing laboratories operating in the state, small size Mrida Parikhyalyas have been established at every block headquarters to cater to greater soil testing needs. These, will enable to issue around 15 lakh soil health cards annually with recommendations balanced fertilizer use.

To supplement the efforts for soil health management Organic Farming is being constantly pursued under the aegis of state organic policy, brought into force during 2018. By now organic farming has been promoted in more than 20800 ha.

There is a programme to extend this further and to around 2 lakh hectares during next five years. Odisha Organic Mission (OOM) will be established as an institutional mechanism to coordinate and complement promotion of organic farming in the state. Organic farming will be scaled up both as a sustainable and economically viable alternate methodology for farmers of Odisha.

In a bid to conserve the indigenous crop varieties, a Gene Bank has been established and 1328 land races (1097 paddy and 231 non paddy varieties) have been collected and being preserved for future use. One paddy variety. Kala Champa has been released and notified by GOI. In the wake of concerns relating to conservation of biodiversity, this endeavor shall supplement all such conservation measures in the state. The preservation effort of local races has recognitions from protection of Plant Varieties Registration Authority (PPVRA).

Courtesy: Department of Agriculture and Farmers Empowerment, Government of Odisha

So, this was the few information, initiatives, achievements and development of agriculture sector of Odisha. Which tells the story of a prosperous Odisha of today and showcasing the golden bright future of Odisha's farmers. And all this became possible only because of one person's hard work, strong determination, visionary decisions and tremendous leadership. *Mr. Naveen Patnaik. The Hon'ble Chief Minister of Odisha.*

❖ **<u>Sports:</u>**

Sports…!

Odisha, Mr. Naveen Patnaik and Hockey. There is very deep connection between these three. As this chapter progresses, the secret of how these three are connected to each other will be revealed. You guys will definitely enjoy the secret that how Odisha has a connection with hockey and hockey's deep connection with Naveen Patnaik. And I think there is no need to tell what connection Naveen Patnaik has with Odisha. We will get to know the deep bonding of these three in this chapter.

India's poorest state will ever be able to make India proud in front of the UN. By spending crores of rupees the country will be able to get medals in Olympics. Will be able to create new world records every time in Guinness Book of World. Yes of course, we are talking about Odisha.

Yes, in the last few years, a lot has been done in Odisha due to which not only the people of Odisha but the entire nation feels proud of it. There would be many such people among us who would be unaware that it is huge proud of not only for our state but for the entire country. Odisha has set the record of building the world's highest capacity hockey stadium.

Actually, we are focusing so much on hockey because it relates not only with this chapter but with the persona also whose biography is being written. There is a huge contribution between hockey and Odisha's transformation to each other.

The Hockey, which India had completely forgotten. Hockey's history was not like this. Hockey has a very golden history in India.

Let's start our story from the year 1936. Adolf Hitler was in power in Germany. The 1936 Olympic games were being held in the German capital, Berlin. It was the final match of hockey between Indian versus Germany. India's Men's hockey team seemed a bit nervous. Because

Germany had defeated them in a previous match. But India had a special player. Who was known as the Wizard among them. The name of the player was Dhyan Chand, Major Dhyan Chand.

India played a fast-paced game. Germany tried its best to win. But Germany could score only one goal against India. On the other hand, India scored 8 goals against Germany. Three of the goals were scored by Dhyan Chand only. This was a very historic game. Impressed by Dhyan Chand's performance, Adolf Hitler offered German citizenship to Dhyan Chand. Going as far as saying that he would be given a position in the German army. But Dhyan Chand wasn't one to bow down to a dictator.

Dhyan Chand did not hesitate to tell Adolf Hitler that *"India is not for sale"*. It was during the prize distribution ceremony, that the whole stadium went silent after listening this words from Dhyan Chand. People were afraid that the fearless reply might lead to Hitler shooting Dhyan Chand. But fortunately, it wasn't so. Rather, Hitler was even more impressed by Dhyan Chand. In fact, this *"Wizard of Hockey"* title to Dhyan Chand, was given to him by Hitler.

What a fascinating story!

Believe it or not, friends, this was our third consecutive Olympics Gold medal in hockey. Perhaps, what may be even more unbelievable is that the Indian hockey team went on to win 5 more Gold medals. At this stage, India was literally the world champion of hockey.

Dhyan Chand, the Wizard's story reached schools, were told to kids at their homes. His stories reached far and wide in the country. And we, as Indians, were very proud of our hockey players.

This was just a glimpse of the golden history of Indian Hockey. Let's come back to the present.

Sports is usually defined as an organized, a competitive and a skillful physical activity which asks for devotion and fair play.

But along with this, apart from being a game, a physical activity, we can also say sports is a definition of fame. You go to any corner of the world, people project every player of any sports as a hero, people treated as a celebrity to a sports person. Be it a football player, hockey player, cricketer or any athlete. People always love players, admire them and respect them. Along with a lot of money, name and fame also become slave to any sports person. It is a great way to earn fame in the world.

And one great truth is that, that success and fame does not belong only to the player but rather the success and fame of the player is also belong to his family, his state and his country too. Mr. Naveen Patnaik understand this fact very well.

It is a matter of pride for us the people of Odisha that, this time Hockey World cup's splendid opening ceremony being held at Cuttack's Barabati Stadium. Hon'ble chief Minister of Odisha Mr. Naveen Patnaik, Central Sports Minister Anurag Thakur and Hockey India's President Dilip Tirkey were also present in the grand opening ceremony. From January 13th 2023 to 29th January 2023, all the matches of this world cup were held in the capital of Odisha Bhubaneswar and Rourkela. Even though the popular game of the people of India today is cricket but hockey has the distinction of being the national game of India.

Today's young generation is probably unaware of this, the dominance we have over world cricket today, the same dominance was existed in hockey too. The Indian hockey team has also expressed the hope with its recent performance that we are once again taking steps towards repeating the golden past of Indian hockey.

In such a faded situation, organizing a tournament like the World Cup in India is certainly a matter of pride for the entire nation. And along with this, this is also a great opportunity to prove ourselves as the uncrowned king of hockey.

But do you know how big a role Odisha has in this revival of hockey? Yes, Odisha has done the miracle of giving hockey its identity back once again. But how did Odisha do that? Which model adopted by the Naveen Government, that hockey got a new fly again?

If India has performed well in men's and women's hockey in the last few years and has raised the name of our country Internationally. So the contribution of Odisha and Odisha's beloved CM Naveen Patnaik for achieving this success will be written in golden letters in the page of history. Odisha has been promoting hockey since 2018 and sponsoring it.

This is the result of the efforts made by the Government of Odisha for Indian Hockey since last few years is that we have got a great opportunity to organize the Hockey World Cup for the second consecutive time. And before this its result was also seen in Tokyo Olympics. Where the Indian Hockey Men's Team won the bronze medal. And ended the medal drought that had been going on for four decades. At the same time, the performance of the Indian Women's Hockey Team was also excellent. With their performance, they managed to make a place in all the Indian's heart.

At that time, the Naveen Government had given a reward of Rs. 10 lakhs each for the players who performed brilliantly in the Olympics. In our country full and packed of cricket lovers, where all other sports have less importance than cricket. Where the cricket craze is at its peak. Where few people give the status of Sports God to Sachin Tendulkar and Mahendra Singh Dhoni. In such circumstances, Odisha's support and involvement for hockey is really a very commendable initiative.

This initiative of Odisha was praised not only by the Government of India. In fact, this initiative was praised all over the world.

Odisha's Chief Minister Naveen Patnaik had said in 2018 that *"This is a gift from the state to the country"*. And Mr. Patnaik said that here our children learn to walk with hockey sticks. This game is a way of life for the people of my state Odisha.

What I had said in the beginning of this chapter that Odisha, Naveen Patnaik and Hockey have a very deep relationship with each other. I think it's time to reveal one of those secrets. And the secret is that CM Naveen Patnaik's love for hockey is not new. Very few people know that when he was studying in The Doon School, Dehradun. Mr. Naveen Patnaik was not just a player of School Hockey Team. He was in a major role of the team.

Yes, Mr. Patnaik was the Goal keeper of The Doon School's Hockey Team. And this precious sports spirit he have inherited from his father Mr. Biju Patnaik. Because the former Chief Minister Mr. Biju Patnaik was a very talented football player during his College days. And the most interesting thing is that Biju Babu was also the Goalkeeper of Ravenshaw College's Football Team. So, Naveen Babu has inherited this quality from his beloved father Biju Babu. So in this way Naveen Babu has a very deep connection with sports.

Ok, after revealing this secret lets come back to our chapter and let us know which model does Odisha adopted which made the fortunes of hockey shine again.

Actually, we all have heard and read that India was once a power house in World Hockey. There was a time when India used to dominate the Olympics.

Indian National Men's Hockey Team has won a total of 8 gold medals in the Olympics so far. Out of which 6 were won continuously only from 1928 to 1956. India also won the Hockey World Cup Final in 1975. But by the end of the 80s, the magic of hockey also started to end in India.

There are many factors behind this like Astroturf Installation and internal politics, due to which there was a continues decline has been seen in the performance of Indian Hockey Team. Due to lack of exposer to any kind of league, even though some good performances were being done, the team was not able to maintain them further. People had started believing that Indian Dominance in hockey was just a thing of the past. And now India has no future in this game. Gradually, the spectators as well as the players were becoming disillusioned with the game.

Meanwhile, the Indian Premier League (IPL) for cricket started in 2008. Many new players and old players got a chance to play cricket again, in IPL. Seeing the success of IPL, Hockey India League was also started. During this period, the Naveen Government shows some interest in hockey and took some important steps for the hockey team.

When this league started in 2013, the government of Odisha bought a team in this league. The team was named Kalinga Lancers. At that time, apart from Barabati Stadium in Cuttack, there was no top class facility in the state for sports. As soon as the Hockey India League started, investment in hockey related infrastructure also started in the state.

The state secretaries *Mr. V.K. Pandian, Mr. Vishal K. Dev* and *Mr. R. Vineel Krishna* also has played a very important role in taking forward this dream and vision of The Hon'ble Chief Minister Mr. Naveen Patnaik for hockey. As hockey's infrastructure started being built in the state, the Naveen government also started to host the International tournaments in the state. And it started with FIH's Hockey Championship Trophy in 2014. Odisha hosted the Champions Trophy in 2014. During this period, a series was also played against Japan at Kalinga Stadium in Bhubaneswar.

Odisha was the only state where the state government had its own club team, Kalinga Lancers, in the Hockey India League. Relations between

Odisha and Hockey India were gradually developing. Along with this, the Naveen Government has started many programs to identify players and develop the players at the grassroots level.

Every step was being taken with excellent preparation and a well thought out strategy. And anyway, the land of Odisha has produced many great players in the past too. Odisha has produced 69 International players only in hockey.

According to their intention, The Naveen Government included the ex-players of hockey in the program from the very beginning. For example, former Indian Hockey captain Dilip Tirkey is heading many communities and councils in the state to develop players at the grassroots level. Today, Indian Men's hockey team's vice-captain Birendra Lakra and Indian women's hockey team's vice-captain Deep Grace, both are from Odisha.

The trend of simultaneously event hosting also continued. And in 2017, Odisha hosted the final of the Hockey World League. It received a lot of praise at national and international level for hosting this tournament. But Naveen Babu was not satisfied with this. The Government of Odisha was thinking of doing something even bigger than this. The Hon'ble Chief Minister Naveen Patnaik was looking for a way to promote hockey in a giant way in the state.

The opportunity that Naveen Babu was looking for has finally arrived. When Sahara withdrew from sponsoring the Indian hockey team in 2018 due to their internal issues in the company. And at that time no private company was coming forward to sponsor hockey. Understanding the urgency of the occasion, Indian hockey team's former captain and BJD's Rajya Sabha Member Dilip Tirkey suggested CM Naveen Patnaik to sponsor the Indian hockey team. On accepting this suggestion, Odisha government joined hands with Indian Hockey and sponsor it.

However, at many places people criticized also after knowing that Odisha is sponsoring National Hockey team. That how can such a backward and poor state could take such huge decision. Actually, there was no precedent for any state in India becoming a sponsor of an official team.

But when once the Naveen government decided to move ahead, then they didn't look back again. After this, the government of Odisha made a deal of Rs 100 crores with Hockey India to sponsor the hockey team for the next 5 years. Odisha government did not stop here. This deal has now been increased to Rs 150 crores. And there has been agreement of supporting the team for the next 10 years.

Apart from the development of basic infrastructure about Rs 140 crores spent on Men's and women's, senior and junior's national team in 5 years by Odisha government. Let us tell you that this is the first time in the history that a state government was sponsoring any game.

And then came the eagerly awaited day. And finally with this, for the first time in 2018, Odisha hosted the 14th World-cup Men's Hockey Tournament. All its matches were played at Kalinga Stadium in the capital Bhubaneswar. Another great step was taken in the year 2019.

The Government of Odisha established *"Odisha Naval Tata Hockey High Performance Center"* (ONTH-HPC) in collaboration with Tata Group. When the first residential batch of this center was announced, there were 30 girls and 31 boys in it. There are more 12 grassroots centers under this center, where more than 2,500 children are being trained.

The main objective of all these centers is to find good talents from grassroots level and move them forward. Apart from this, providing them all kinds of facilities like their training is done properly. And providing them with everything they need should also be included in their priority.

Apart from Grassroots Performance Center, Naveen Government has also started promoting such areas where there are a lots of players but due to lack of proper facilities, not all players could advance.

Sundargarh is one of the 30 districts of Odisha. Many legendary Indian players like Pramod Teeka, Dilip Tirkey, Jyoti Sunita Kullu, Rajesh Balla and Niyamit Topo have come from this district. After all, Sundargarh is the center fort of hockey in Odisha. And now very soon it is going to become Indian Hockey's Hub. For this, Synthetic Hockey Turf is being installed by the government of Odisha in 70 blocks of the districts. So that the young talented players get used to playing on turf from the beginning.

Along with this, Odisha hosted FIH men's Series Final and Olympic Hockey Qualifier 2019, 2020 FIH Pro league too. This was the result of so many years of hard work and struggle of Naveen government that Odisha got the opportunity to host the Hockey World Cup for the second time too.

For this, Odisha government decided to organize the tournament in Bhubaneswar and Rourkela. And as a result today India's largest and extremely modern hockey stadium exists in Rourkela. 20,000 people can watch the match at a time in the stadium, prepared at a cost of Rs 112 crores.

This 15-acres of complex has many international facilities like Athletic Track, Football Ground, Basketball Court, Volleyball Court, Swimming Pool, Aquatic Complex, Yoga Hall, and Medical Room.

This stadium is named after the tribal leader Birsa Munda. This reveals another transparent and clear intentions of the Naveen Government.

This vision of Odisha Government is not just for hockey, also for other games. Like Odisha government is sponsoring under-15 and under-18 teams in football, and along with this an MOU has been signed with rugby India in 2020 under which Odisha government the government of Odisha will sponsor the Rugby India for a certain period.

Puri, one of the most famous city of Odisha, is known for its wrestling heritage. Today, a Residential Academy is being built there for wrestling and cricket. Similarly, Indore Stadium have been built in Ganjam and Baharamgarh, the home of weight lifting. The Naveen Government is identifying and developing local audience under this model.

This is a master stroke of the Government of Odisha. This increases the interest of the local audience and brings out good talents even more. And one important thing is that by hosting the Hockey World Cup in Odisha, it gave strength to the youth here and their interest towards the game increased. Recognizing the important role of the Odisha Government in the success of the Indian Hockey Team, the Indian Government has set a target of joining the top-10 in the Olympics by 2028.

For this, the Government of India has adopted this model of the Government of Odisha and has also requested other states of India to sponsor and promote at least on sport. So that by 2028 the number of players representing India in the Olympics can triple. This will increase the chances of winning medals in Olympic. And India will become a global power in the world of sports.

In this way, Odisha has made an important contribution in the revival of the national game hockey. And many players from the state were representing India in the hockey today.

Hockey is a very important part of the sports culture of Odisha and the people of the state also like this game much.

Odisha wants to bring back the glory of Indian Hockey. For this reason, every possible help and support is being given to hockey from Naveen

Government. With these efforts and steps of the Hon'ble Chief Minister Mr. Naveen Patnaik, the image of Odisha, which was known for poverty and natural disasters, has been wiped and destroyed to a great extent.

It is the result of these efforts of Mr. Naveen Patnaik that Odisha is improving its tarnished image. Along with economic growth, fame also increasing. Mr. Naveen Patnaik's works are being praised not only in India but all over the world. Political opponents are also bound to praise Naveen Babu's good governance and policies.

From a common man to the Prime Minister of the country Mr. Narendra Damodardash Modi is praising the work of Naveen Babu. Be it print media or electronic media, it is full packed of praises for Mr. Naveen Patnaik.

"Odisha won the Sportstar Aces Award for the beat state for the promotion of Sports at the Taj Mahal Palace in Mumbai. Odisha Chief Minister Naveen Patnaik graced the occasion and received the award from India batting great Sunil Gavaskar and Suresh Nambath, Editor of The Hindu".

Courtesy: **Sportstar**

"The story of the Odisha sports model is inspiring not just for other states but many countries. The success lies in uplifting the quality of sports right from the grassroots level so that the players get all the facilities at a very young age. With all the efforts put in the last decade, Odisha will have a long-lasting impact on the rich sporting heritage of India and it will act as a pioneer in the sporting revolution of the country".

Courtesy: **Kreedon**

"Odisha's rise as a shining example for sports infra. Odisha's massive investment in sport infrastructure goes beyond Bhubaneswar and is spread across the state. The statessh sports budget in 2023-24 is Rs 1,300 crore, the highest in India".

Courtesy: **Hindustan Times**

"Odisha's accession to becoming the sports powerhouse of the country can be hailed as a successful model for the rest of the states in the country to follow".

Courtesy: **The Bridge**

"Odisha Government has bagged the prestigious Best State Promoting Sports Award at the FICCI India Sports Awards 2019 held at New Delhi".

Courtesy: **The New Indian Express**

"Investment in sports is an investment in youth and investment in youth is an investment in the future". The **Hon'ble Chief Minister Mr. Naveen Patnaik** *said.* This is one of the best golden lines among the many golden words of Naveen Babu.

6 – Odisha – Naveen, Naveen – Odisha, A Role Model

Naveen Patnaik, the name of a great public leader, who used to write his passion, his experience through his pen's point, a soft spoken person and a true gentle man. Today he has turned into a *"Chanakya"* in politics. In his every political move, there is a lesson, not only for his supporters but also for his opponents.

Whether the situation is adverse or favorable, he has a way to deal with it in a controllable manner. He has his own polite, soft and wise way to face the situation. He is such an invincible leader of India that not only his opponents but even the natural disasters have surrendered in front of him. The whole world is imitating Naveen Babu's *'0' Casualty Mission.* Naveen's prior, quick and effective plans are able to challenge the natural disasters that Odisha has been facing through the last couple of years.

A world-class writer with no sharp political edges. Today, he has turned into a splendid and un-parallel politician. Neither his father, the great leader Mr. Biju Patnaik nor any of his family members had ever thought that Naveen Patnaik would stand as an unsurmountable leader in the politics of Odisha, all the political analyzers and pundits are bound to accept this. Even at the national level, there is no popular leader like him.

After Biju Babu's death, he is an unrivalled ruler of Odisha today. Even at this age, the people of Odisha are preferring to see him as their leader. People are willing to see him in the throne always. Winning elections again and again is not the measure of success.

Winning people's heart repeatedly is the true and biggest criterion. Handling things strategically and staying in power for such a long time is a new record. Also, politically he almost doesn't have any opponents. In Odisha, no political leader and no political party has experienced such a situation ever before.

It has been more than 25 years that he is running the state successfully. He took over the rule of Odisha for such a long period of time but in all these years, no luxurious change was seen in his lifestyle and behavior. He always stays clean shaved, his identity includes wearing a very simple slipper with white Kurta Pajama. He prefers to eat very simple home cooked food. Showing power to people or being abusive is not involved in his character at all. Even he is very soft and polite towards his political opponents.

This is the reason why whatever allegations his opponents make against him has no effect on the people of Odisha. That's why there has been no decrease in the love and trust of the people of Odisha on Naveen Babu.

He believes 4.5 crores of people of Odisha are his family. Extraordinary personality, emotional nature, there are many terms for the introduction of Naveen. Naveen Patnaik, who lived his life considering Biju Babu as his ideal since childhood, had developed humanitarian concerns within him. After entering politics, Naveen Patnaik has been following public service as his religion. He has been always standing with 4.5 crores of Odia in their every happiness and sorrow.

In 1999, that super cyclone had created such a ruckus in Odisha, the plight, the worst situation of the state and its people had saddened him to such an extent that he prepared a special blueprint to counter this disaster, **'0' Causality Mission.** Till today he is carrying on with this mission and has been fighting with these disasters. As a result of which, after the super cyclone of 1999, Odisha faced the natural disaster almost every year. But the Naveen Government and the people of great state Odisha fight with natural calamities with their 56" inches chests exposed.

That terrible dark night of October 1999 was not less than any horrible, horrendous dream. But it was not a dream, it was a reality.

India had completed 50 years of its glorious Independence. Odisha had completed more than 60 years of gaining the recognition as an

Independent State. In 1999, October the super cyclone came, from the Government to the general public, no one was ready for this. A large piece of land of Odisha got destroyed badly due to the devastation of this super cyclone. The state Government was just watching like a spectator, helplessly at the time of this orgy of nature. When the people were suffering and pleading for help, at that time even the state government seemed helpless and was pleading for help.

How can a helpless government take up the responsibilities of its citizens?

But within one year, from 1999-2000 everything changed in the state!

Odisha came out from the burden of fear and helplessness and stood up with its exposed chest to encounter the natural disaster. The ordinary Odia people started standing up and the government also started standing up.

How did this miracle happen…?

After the year 1999, many times the storms ruined the chest and heart of Odisha state, there have been floods many times, and many times the cyclone and earthquake had come.

But the one man's strong conviction and call *'O' casualty* defeated even the natural disaster too. And the man is Odisha's popular Chief Minister Naveen Patnaik.

Naveen Patnaik's life till now was not associated with any politics or political events. The only thing connected with him was that he was the youngest son of Biju Patnaik, the former Chief Minister of Odisha. But after stepping in politics at the age of 50, he is providing a great leadership in such a way that why only the flood and cyclone, he has succeeded in changing the complete face of Odisha. Beginning from blooming smiles in the face of an ordinary laborers to in the field of introducing our state at world forum, he has made successful efforts. There is a huge heaven and earth difference between 2000's Odisha and today's Odisha.

A state Odisha, un-progressed in economic field, unorganized in operating economic systems, today Odisha has converted into a role model for not only other states but also for the whole country in economic development and growth.

The Central Government equally follows the schemes of Odisha Government. Recently, administrators from 6 states had come to Odisha to understand and learn about Odisha's cyclone operating model.

The United Nation appreciated Odisha government's preparedness in dealing with the very very severe cyclone Phailin, saying it would be a highlight for studying the efforts as a successful case study globally. Terming the evacuation of nearly one million people, which ensured minimal loss of human lives, a 'landmark success story', special representative of the UN secretary general for disaster risk reduction *Margareta Wahistrom* told to TOI. *"We are very impressed. We have plans to use it as a model for other cities and countries to follow as part of our global efforts on disaster risk reduction"*. Margareta Wahlstrom added. According to *The Times of India*.

Isn't it a matter of pride…?

After the super cyclone of 1999, Odisha faces floods, cyclone and draught almost every year. Similarly, in the year 2013 Phailin cyclone was the most terrible. Only in Ganjam district, where Cyclone Phailin made its landfall, almost 200,000 houses and 200,000 hectares of agriculture land got damaged.

But the big thing is that the state government stood with the people, not even an inch was step back from the people in these circumstances.

The way Naveen Government dealt with this natural disaster and prepared decorated bed for his people was really an inspiration for others.

The UN praised Hon'ble Chief Minister Naveen Patnaik for his "well-resourced disaster management authority" that saves lives during natural calamities. In an interview to The Times of India, Mami Mizutori, chief of UN office for disaster risk reduction (UNDRR) said, Odisha's example gives important lessons on "strengthening disaster risk governance, investing in preparedness and scenario planning while spreading a greater understanding of disaster risk".

Isn't it a matter of pride…?

"Every life is so precious". Naveen Babu feels and experiences this each and every moment. After Phailin in 2013, Hud-Hud Cyclone 2014, in 2018 Titli, in 2019 Fany, again in 2019 Bulbul, in 2020 Affan, Yash in 2021. During all these major natural disaster, due to the excellent leadership, prior preparation and early steps of Naveen government, the slogan **'0' casualty** has been successful.

As part of the cyclonic operation, evacuating and transporting safely people from the cyclone prone areas to safe areas. Moved lakhs of people to safe place before the arrival of cyclone, to provide them shelter, and provide them cooked food is not an easy job.

The administration in the cyclone prone districts has fallen into such structure that they have been doing this work very easily, smoothly and efficiently. It is said that innovative leadership, strong determination and futuristic thought is the key to success for such circumstances.

The Naveen Government fasten the waistline belts to fight with these natural calamities and prepared the system for long term and made them so strong in all aspects. All the state governments used to demand immediately financial support and assistance for the disaster in front of the central government.

But during the yaas cyclone, the Naveen government set an amazing example. The Naveen Government didn't demand a single rupee in front of the central government to fulfill the loss occurred because of yaas cyclone, rather he put forward a proposal to the central government to support the futuristic long term scheme.

Such a futuristic and dedicated leadership can be seen only in a capable leader. Cyclone, flood, draught are the friends forever for Odisha. The farmers always face such natural calamities and due to which they had to fall in many financial crises always. Farmers and farming is the back bone of Odisha. Along with improving the financial condition of the farmers, to remove the fear of natural disasters within the farmer, the Naveen Government launched an innovative scheme *"Kalia Yojana"*. Through this, farmers got direct financial assistance from the state government. As a result, the economic condition of a farmer is also improving.

People say that Naveen Patnaik, who set foot at the age of 77, used to be very travel loving guy in his youth. He loves to travel the world. But it is very surprising that apart from going to Delhi for government works, he didn't left Odisha and gone anywhere since last more than two decades. Yes, it is true that he went to London only once in 2012 for his treatment.

His immense love for Odisha, development of Odisha, always concerned for the progress of the people of Odisha is the reason for which he buried his travelling desire.

A natural disaster prone state, and in disaster time, Naveen Patnaik has started his political journey in such a disaster situation. When the issue of organizing disaster comes to the fore, to evacuate people during disaster, the state government's own ODRAP team formed in the NDRF framework comes first into mind.

Soldiers of ODRAP, along with going to the affected areas and rescuing people in an emergency situation and providing them relief goods, they play a vital role in such situations. Not only that, cutting trees from roads, removing electricity pols from road in collaboration with state's fire fighting force men and police has been appreciated widely.

Mr. Naveen Patnaik after coming to power in 2000, formed the ODRAF in 2001. Odisha was the first in a region to form such a force at the state level in the entire country.

Similarly, for the people living in the 480 km coastal areas of Odisha. A system called EWTS was started for the first time in the country by the Odisha Government in the month of April 2018 to deliver natural disasters forecasting information. People are also becoming alert and prepared to face the disaster after getting advance information.

In the 1999 super cyclone, more than 10,000 people died. And the main reason for this orgy of death was that no such information could reach to the people in time. People had no weather information of any kind. But now more than 1200 villages under more than 25 blocks of districts like Balasore, Bhadrak, Jagatsinghpur, Puri and Ganjam are included in the system. At a distance of 1.5 kilometers from the sea, 122 watch towers have been constructed so far. Informations about cyclone and Tsunami are given through sirens from all these watch towers. Another major contribution to Odisha's natural disaster section is the multipurpose cyclone rest shelters.

It would not be a mistake to say that all this is the brain child of Hon'ble CM Mr. Naveen Patnaik. Odisha has many more programs related to Odisha's cyclone operating system and to deal with such disasters. What I mean to say is that, all these schemes are an embodiment of the loving spirit of the Odia people.

A leader who does not love his state and his people from the bottom of his heart will never be able to do this or achieve so much success. The people of Odisha will never forget the man, the leader who saved the Odia people from natural calamities like flood, storm, draught and cyclone etc.

That's why Mr. Naveen Patnaik has earned the distinction of becoming a Chief Minister for five consecutive times.

A leader always protects his followers and it is this quality that makes him an excellent and splendid leader and turns him into a role model.

That's why Naveen Patnaik will always be Great Leader, unparalleled persona in the social, political and economic history of Odisha, and this is a truth!

For the service of people, the one who is always ahead is called a true leader and Naveen Patnaik is an example of this.

His every moment is filled with thoughtfulness!

His every plan is fruitful!

If we say that he has Midas touch in his hands!

A story is compiled in his touch!

Politics gets a new vibrant look!

Role Model…!

Mission '0' Casualty:

29th October 1999, A black day for Odisha. The super cyclone caught in a complete state of unawareness and unpreparedness, also the state had never seen wind speed of over 300 km per hour. No one across Odisha had any clue of what preparations were required. Even IMD's predicted technologies were too primitive.

There were no warnings, no plan of evacuations, no safe buildings for shelter, no relief. The super cyclone ravaged over half the state. Snatching away more than ten thousand human lives. Besides millions in animal casualties. From that day when the state was to reduce to being a mute spectator to total demonstration to till today when such cyclone still continues to lash Odisha regularly.

But the body count has been successfully brought down to the double digit and off late to almost to '0' casualties, has been nothing sort of a miracle. Leadership is, what make the difference. Strong, clear minded, visionary leadership. Mr. Naveen Patnaik took over the rains as the Chief Minister of Odisha and since then things have been looked up and better. Odisha has always been to prone to natural disasters, taking lesson from this fact, the Hon'ble Chief minister of Odisha realized that, this needs an intense preparedness, right down to the grass root level. We can't stop these natural disasters from occurring but we definitely can prepare ourselves to fight them and that's exactly what he has let the state to do.

His *Every life is precious* motto leading to adopting a strict "Zero casualty" mission has kept the administration across all levels at tenocks. Make them responsible as well as responsive. Over two decades of learning has now been rolled into improving response capacity. Precision planning and emasculated implementation. This coupled with robust institutional frame work, strong community level participation of all stake holder and capacity development has strengthened the state's ability to deal with the situation.

The first step to Odisha's world class disaster management system was to become self-reliant. On 29th December 1999 the OSDMA (Odisha State Disaster Management Authority) was formed. Followed by the policy to fight natural disaster at the national front the NDA was formed six years later. Subsequent to that Odisha also established, The Odisha Disaster Rapid Action Force (ODRAF) in 2001. This was the first such state level response team across India.

In fact, the NDRF was formed much later. Beyond this, it was always realized that simply forming a response team won't stop the problem. In forming an orient in the masses on how to effectively fight such calamities together were also required. Resultly community level capacity was strengthened. So as to not make them not dependent on the government every time.

Right from gram panchayat, to blocks to districts on the state level are robust frame work laid on how to fight the calamities together, effectively. Which is still a much need confidence and fighting spirit in every one.

This is also been aided by empowering the panchayatiraaj institutions and women self-help groups to strengthened local and districts administrations inding with pre and during disaster rescues, evacuation, first aid training, shelter management, relief operations and early recovering actions.

Hand in hand all elected representatives, right from the honorable Chief Minister himself to the chief secretary to all word members, right down to the lowest level functionaries are all being trained in various aspects of disaster management. The Odisha State Disaster Management Authority on its end has been making use state of art of technologies in forecast early warning disseminations, monitoring rescue operations, rehabilitation, damage assessment and reconstruction.

Resultantly the state robust institutional capacity has been helping the state take timely decisions with respect to operations management, keeping people in the center of every act. That by a strong visionary leadership keeping a close watch on the operations and developments, guided by the central philosophy of saving every life.

Not only have all panchayats been empowered, till now over 23,000 villages have trained to fight such natural calamities. Over 1000 cyclone and flood centers have been built across the state. Equipped with 32 types of equipment and machines, such as DG sets, First Aid kits, wood cutters and many more to help ground level communities prepare better for disasters, roads, electricity, housing are made cyclone proof and flood proof.

The state government is investing heavily in makings its coastal power barrier disaster resistance. The state is also maximizing the concrete housing. Due to which evacuation across coastal villages have been substantially reduced. The state government is also strengthening the capacity of all fire service stations right down till the block level. Post cyclone psycho-social counselling is also provided to people, who been unable to deal with the trauma.

Its noteworthy that Odisha is not only the first state in India, it also the first state across 18 Indian oceanic nations to be Tsunami prepared states. In fact, two villages have been UNESCO Certified as Tsunami ready. Within the next one year 388 villages will be Tsunami ready. As a result, despite facing six cyclones in just the last three years, including three summer cyclones.

The state has continued to demonstrate its development capacity in meet a getting such disaster. When this extremely severe cyclone hit Odisha 2019, over one million people were evacuated within 24 hours flat. And astounding an unmatched record in human evacuation.

A state with sought help from its neighboring states in 1999 is now sending its disaster experts to multiple Indian states. Like, West Bengal, Andhra Pradesh, Kerala, Bihar and Meghalaya. Never the less on lot more of such result oriented efforts are still required.

When it comes to long term disaster resilants infrastructure for meeting at on the adverse impact of disaster. Not only on human lives but also on rebuilding livelihoods. With this anying the state government has even started main streaming disaster risk reduction into the government frame work of every department.

Such effort has been fetching international Loral's and acclaims for Odisha, including the United Nations. The appreciation with its resilient leadership, along with the state governments consistent efforts, the state marches on towards not just been a model state for the nation but for the entire world.

Role Model...!

Mission Shakti:

'Mission Shakti' is not just a slogan, Mission Shakti is a life stream, Mission Shakti is a movement with a powerful momentum that has grown beyond its stated vision. Mission Shakti touching lives not only of the women it serves, but also of the families, communities, and societies they live in. Mission Shakti is writing a new history of development of Odisha.

By looking down on one caste, one gender and ignoring them and suppressing them. It is very easy to say that their life and life stream is begin from the kitchen stove to the rice vessels. At best, the business of pickles, papad, incense sticks or lending money in interest in the village will remain limited. If we were thinking like this, then we were thinking wrong.

Mobility is empowerment, if a woman has her mobility in her hands, if she goes out of her house. To attend a meeting or for her some personal work. Only then she will feel herself empowered.

The whole vision of the Hon'ble Chief Minister is that; women will come out of the kitchen. Their voices will be heard outside. They will be able to participate as a decision maker in the public space. Mr. Naveen Patnaik's vision.

The contribution of women and youth generation towards a healthy society and nation building is incredible. If women move forward then society will forward, the country will progress and Mr. Naveen Patnaik understands this very well. Naveen Patnaik has been able to make women self-reliant through 'Mission Shakti'. No house, no society, no state or not any country can progress without the empowerment of women. Mr. Naveen Patnaik had feels and understood this in the beginning itself.

Mr. Naveen Patnaik had also said about respect for women along with work for villages. This Mission Shakti was launched in the state on 8th March 2001 on the eve of International women's day. And the tremendous thing is that in the last 23-24 years, more than 80 lakh women have joined Mission Shakti.

Mission Shakti has been able to make women self-reliant. During Covid-19 times, the entire state has seen and witnessed the work of women's self-help group. Apart from being self-reliant, they also being able to participate in the development of the state.

Now there is even an independent department for Mission Shakti in the Government of Odisha.

Similarly, a historic decision was taken in 2011 to provide 50% reservation for women in Panchayati Raaj departments. Such decisions of Mr. Naveen Patnaik have brought a huge change in the social and economic status of women in the entire state.

To reserve 33% seats for women in the Legislative Assembly and the Lok Sabha, a resolution was passed by the Serb committee in the Legislative Assembly and Lok Sabha. He didn't just stop at the proposal. In the general election of 2019, women were made candidates for 7 seats out of 21 Lok Sabha seats.

Mission Shakti was started in 2001 in efforts of Hon'ble Chief Minister Mr. Naveen Patnaik. Mr. Naveen Patnaik had only one focus at that time, that the women who are living in a corner of their house, confined to her kitchen only. How will those women will find an independent identity for themselves?

How will they have their own identity? How women will live with respect in society? Keeping all these things in mind Mr. Naveen Patnaik started Mission Shakti.

At that time when this Mission Shakti was started, many people were doing research amid a lot of uncertainty and apprehension, that how the women will connect with this mission and how the work will go on smoothly.

But today it has been more than 23 years, within these 23 years the SHG which was started with few women. At present, a strong force of more than 80 lakh women is ready in 6 lakh SHG Groups. With a clear objective of empowering women through gainful activities by providing credit and market linkage. Empowerment of women through WSHGs under Mission Shakti is a flagship program of the Naveen Government.

'Mission Shakti'. It would not be a mistake to say that Mission Shakti has transformed into an ocean today. Today it has become a great Role Model.

Every scheme of the Naveen Government has become a *Role Model*!

Every steps of Naveen Government have become a *Role Model*!

In fact, Hon'ble Chief Minister Mr. Naveen Patnaik himself has become an ideal and a *Role Model* in the political history of India!

Let me tell you very fantastic and amazing fact, that the meaning of this word 'Naveen' is new and role model.

So, whose name itself means role model. Who can stop him from being a role model…?

Role Model…! Role Model…! Role Model…!

7 – Odisha Millets Mission

The amount of power in three glasses of milk, the same power is present in this one glass of '*Mandia*'. The amount of calcium you get by drinking three glasses of milk, one glass of millet contains more calcium than that.

Now a day, if you ask an elderly person the secret of his good health, they will tell that in their childhood their parents used to feed them millets in large quantities. This is the reason why even at this age they are still so healthy and fit.

But with passing time all this super food has disappeared from our society and our plates. Now a day's people are abandoning this super healthy food and enjoying this new age junk food to make themselves feel modern and proud. But on the other hand, due to this type of eating habits, they suffer from various types of diseases.

Millets are part of the traditional staple diet and crop systems in Odisha supplementing nutritional needs of the communities, especially in the rainfed regions. Millets are one of the most valuable and nutrive ingredient among all agricultural crops. The conscious pursuit of an agricultural policy since the 1960s to meet national food security with paddy and wheat has led to a decline in millet production and consumption. Millets were not the focus crops in food security framework of the green revolution.

Millets have numerous health benefits. Millets is rich in niacin, which is important for healthy skin and organ function. Millets are low-glycemic index foods and can help keep your blood sugar from spiking after you eat. Millets are full of soluble fiber, which trap fat in your gut and can lower the cholesterol level in your blood. That can help reduce your chances of heart diseases. Millets are good sources of magnesium too, which may prevent heart failure. Millet is rich in protein and calcium and has more essential amino acids than most other cereals. They're also gluten-free, so people with celiac disease or gluten sensitivities can enjoy them.

Despite of all these features and health benefits, despite of so many blessings and which is easiest to cultivate compared to other crops. Millets seemed to have sunk somewhere for many decades. People had completely forgotten millet. But the commendable steps of the Naveen Government revived the millets. This Odisha Millets Mission of Naveen Government has once again revived and included millets in people's lives. This is an excellent decision of the Chief Minister Mr. Naveen Patnaik reign.

Odisha Millets Mission (OMM), is one of a flagship program of Department of Agriculture and farmers' Experiment, Government of Odisha.

Special Program for promotion of millets in Tribal areas of Odisha (Odisha Millets Mission) was launched by Govt of Odisha in 2017 to revive millets in farms and on plates and simultaneously focus on production, processing, consumption, marketing and inclusion of millets in Government schemes. The nutritious millets traditionally occupied substantial part of the diets and crop systems in tribal areas. Millets require less water and are more resilient to climate vulnerability. They can also be cultivated on the undulating and change and be cultivated even in undulating terrain.

Reduction in millets resulted in nutrition deficiency. It led to unsustainable cropping systems increasing demand on water. In order to address growing crop failures and nutritional issues, millets need to be revived. To revive, a flagship program has been launched by the Naveen Government.

The Odisha Government's cabinet recently approved an estimated budget of Rs, 2687.4587 crore for four years (2023-24 to 2026-27 financial years) for the implementation of the special program to promote Odisha Millets Mission.

It emerged from consultation between Government, Academia (NCDS) and civil Society Organizations (RRA Network, ASHA Network and Local NGOs).

It is the first of its kind of agriculture program with a priority on increasing consumption in Odisha. The program aims comprehensive revival of millets in farms and plates to promote climate-resilient farming and contribute to addressing micronutrient deficiency.

The program is implemented through WSHGs/FPOs with the support of NGOs and research institutions with oversight from the Department of Agriculture and Farmers' Empowerment.

In the first phase of implementation (2017-18), the program was operational in 30 blocks across seven districts and is subsequently, expanded to 65 blocks in 11 districts.

In the second and third phases, the program reached out to 84 blocks in 15 districts during the 2021-22. Further, it has been extended to 142 blocks in 19 districts during 2022-23.

Currently, the Odisha Government has increased its area of implementation from 142 blocks in 19 districts to 177 blocks in all 30 districts from 2023-24 onwards. *Courtesy- Pragativadi*

The objectives of Odisha Millets Mission are as follows:

> - Promoting household level consumption
> - Improving productivity of millet crops by improved agronomic practices
> - Promoting FPOs for marketing
> - Setting up decentralized processing unit
> - Inclusion of millets in ICDS, MDM and PDS

Recognition and impact of Odisha Millets Mission:

> - The Government of India has asked all states to adopt Odisha Millets Mission model for promotion of millets, pulses and oilseeds.

- ➢ The state planning commission of Chhattisgarh has asked the Government of Chhattisgarh to start a millet mission on the lines of "Odisha Millets Mission".
- ➢ The Government of India has setup a task force to understand the framework of the Odisha Millets Mission and to revise the National sub mission on millets based on the learnings of the OMM.
- ➢ Cambridge University partnered with Odisha Millets Mission to explore possibility of design of OMM as alternative to Green Revolution framework.
- ➢ The Governor of Maharashtra has asked Government of Maharashtra to explore initiating a project on Millets considering the Odisha Millets Mission.
- ➢ UN-IFAD and UN-FAO have supported the framework of Odisha Millets Mission as suitable for taking up agro-ecological initiatives.

Odisha became the first state to declare direct incentive to farmers for more than three years through DBT.

Odisha became the first state in the country to complete benchmarking of prices of little millet and foxtail millet.

Odisha became first state to develop standard specifications for the minor millet machinery through recognized panel of experts from different scientific institutions.

Odisha received award for best government initiative on millet promotion by MoFPI-IIFPT.

First state to include Ragi laddu in ICDS through support of district Mineral Foundation.

Millet Shakti Cafe: Cafes have been established across Odisha, called Millet Shakti café to serve the millet- based hot cooked items and bakery products. More than 45 events have been organized and millet-based food items have been served to more than 4.4 lakh people in the last few years.

Millets at International Hockey World Cup: As part of its objective to popularize millets in urban areas, the Odisha Millets Mission collaborated with the Trishakti Federation of SHGs promoted by Mission Shakti and a millet-based food stall called "Mandia Café" was put up at the Fan Village inside Kalinga Stadium during the International Hockey World Cup 2018. The members of the Federation managed the café and interacted with the visitors. The women had been trained and technically supported by State Program Secretariat hosted by Naba Krishna Chowdhury center for Development Studies (NCDS), Bhubaneswar.

Packaged and bakery products like biscuits, laddos, muffins and fresh hot-cooked recipes like salad, sandwiches, vada, biryani and kheer were served to audiences and other attendees. Encouraging response was received, especially by families who were looking for healthier options while not compromising on taste.

Through Mandia café, they didn't just provide people with healthy and tasty food but also communicated the nutritional benefits of millets. Having experienced millet recipes, people didn't just eat at the café but also took back biscuits, laddos and other recipes for their family and friends.

The initiative got good media coverage and gave the members of Trishakti skills and opportunity to initiate millet-based enterprises.

Nutritional Security: The objective of Odisha Millets Mission is to revive millets on the farms and on plates. Ragi procurement has supported the consumption among people. The procured Ragi based entitlements were included in the PDS and ICDS Schemes. These efforts are set to be expanded through inclusion of ragi based preparation in MDM. Hence, the focus has been on the nutritionally vulnerable category of children.

Gender and Nutrition Benefits: Mechanized and decentralized processing of millets at a block level has helped increasing ease of doing agriculture and in reducing women's drudgery in producing millets.

Climate Resilience: The assured market for finger millet has led to an increase in area under millet production. This has increased farmer's resilience in the face of drought. Deficient rainfall posed a problem for paddy cultivation but has had no impact on non-paddy crops.

> *The "Special Program for Promotion of Millets in Tribal Areas" being implemented in sprit as the "Odisha Millets Mission" aims at improving nutrition at the household level through revival of millets in farms and on plates. By making investments on improving productivity, processing and a price guarantee for millet crops, millets are being mainstreamed in Odisha. Promotion of millets is also an integral part of the Agriculture Policy of Odisha which aims at providing an income support to farmers.*
>
> *The Government of Odisha is committed to make millet grains and products available at affordable rates to the common man with the support of the enterprising spirit of our Women's Self Help Groups, where necessary.*
>
> *I hope that Odisha's endeavor will inspire the national policy for reviving millet production in the country.*

Shri Naveen Patnaik
Chief Minister, Odisha

Millet is a very ancient food. Because of its extraordinary beneficial effects towards health, it is considered as a super food. At the time when it was about to disappear from our society. The Odisha Government is making every effort for its revival. This step and effort of Naveen Government is definitely praiseworthy. The Government is trying everything possible. Providing every kind of help to farmers in every corner of Odisha.

So, that is why the common people should also participate in this effort of the Government.

If the general public can join this effort of the Government and make it a successful model, then another green revolution will be successful in the country.

Thank You!

8 – 2024 – A Milestone to Achieve

Har Aan Naveen ke Liye Fikar Gulistaan Hai Aaj Kal
Har Saans Aashna Hai Unki Sehat Ke Liye Aaj Kal
Tum Jaan, Tum Shaan, Tum Swabhimaan Ho Odisha Ki
Muntejir Hai Siddat Se Awaam Tumahri Fir, Taaj Poshi Ke Liye Aaj
Kal…!

To be a Great and Popular Leader, it is important and mandatory to have many qualities in you. Out of all those qualities, these four most important qualities mean a lot and they are;

- ✓ Honesty
- ✓ Justice
- ✓ Selfless
- ✓ Courage

After the death of the legendary leader Biju Patnaik, when son Naveen Patnaik launched the Biju Janata Dal, a splinter group of Janata Dal, on 26ᵗʰ December, 1997. The people of Odisha accepted him only as "Biju Babu's" son. Achieving power and holding on to it for more than two decades are two very opposite things.

We can say, he inherited the status from his legendary father. We can say this and it is very easy to say that as the son of Biju Babu, Naveen Patnaik entered into politics. He won the by-election of Aska constituency in 1997 so easily, fine. Formed a party in the name of his father, agree. Became the Chief Minister of the state, that is also fine. But ruling 4.5 crore of people's heart of the state for more than 23 years is no mean feat. Winning people's trust for 23 years and maintaining their faith in you is not an easy thing.

For that you must have **honesty** within yourself, you must have the ability to do **justice**, must have the morale to serve the people completely **selflessly**, and to do all this you must have the **courage**, because a coward person can never take such a big decision.

In these 26-27 years of political journey from 1997 till today, it has been proving that all these qualities are well present in Mr. Naveen Patnaik. It cannot be denied that Naveen Patnaik is filled with all these excellent leadership qualities within him.

Naveen Patnaik has not been accused of even a single penny of corruption in these decades. Not only did he save his hem from the dark stain of corruption but in fact, he did not even spare the person who committed any corruption. Be it a Minister in his cabinet, MLA or any bureaucrats. Mr. Patnaik has done the work with great *honesty* till now. His belief is that Government's money is public money and will be spent only on the public and their welfare. If a person, consider public service as his religion then corruption cannot even come to close to him.

After coming to power, Mr. Patnaik has done *justice* to every section of people in his state. Be it casteism, gender or religion. He never discriminates against anyone. In his eyes, the 4.5 crore people of Odisha are all equal. The best thing about his rule is that during his rule he never encouraged any religious riots in Odisha. The law and order in the state always maintained equally. Health, agriculture, housing, or education related, whatever schemes are initiated by the Naveen government. Full care is taken to ensure that people from every section of the society get maximum benefit from the Yojana without any discrimination.

It has often been seen that people come into politics and spend money to contest election with the intention to earn money, to build properties and increase bank balance for them and their coming generation. Almost leaders and politicians are concerned about how to accumulate as much wealth as possible. But in the Naveen Patnaik's part it is exactly opposite.

He was living a luxurious life before entering politics. But after coming into politics, Naveen simplified his life and lifestyle. Wore very simple clothes like white Pajama, Kurta and slippers, and love to eat very simple home cooked food. Till date no one has heard him abusing, not even his political opponents or showing any sign of power to anyone.

He serves his people of his state with great simplicity and humanity, selflessly. During these decades, he neither gathered any properties for himself nor built a mountain of bank balance nor did he dreamt of a luxurious life. In today's cut throat and greedy political era, it is very rare to see such *selfless* leader Mr. Naveen Patnaik.

In politics, you need *courage* the most when you have to choose one, between power and the people. The same thing happened with Mr. Patnaik. He also had to face a similar strange religious crisis when he had to choose between the people and the power.

In August 2008, Kandhamal witnessed one of the most violent communal riots of the state following the killing of VHP leader Swami Laxmananda Saraswati by Maoists. More than 40 Hindus and Christians were killed during the riots triggered by the murder. More than 600 villages ransacked, over 5,600 houses were looted or burnt down and over 60,000 people were left homeless. According to Wikipedia. A lot more was burnt and destroyed in that mutual tension. There was a big storm in the politics of Odisha too. At that time there was a coalition government of BJD and BJP in the state.

However, the ties between the two parties soured in the aftermath of kandhamal riots. The supremo of Biju Janata Dal Mr. Naveen Patnaik had broken more than a decade-long alliance with the Bharatiye Janata Party without any fear or favor. Without caring that power may also be lost from his hands. And that is a different thing that the move proved later a political masterstroke as it strengthened his secular credential. You need a lot of *courage* to take this kind of decisions. Naveen Patnaik shows his courage and decided in favor of the public without caring about power. And distanced himself from a big political party like BJP.

That's why despite his accented Odiya and somewhat deficient oratorical skills, Mr. Patnaik has a special place in voters' hearts.

But today the situation of state politics in Odisha is very different. Today the opposition seems to be getting stronger.

Ruben Banerjee writes in his book *'Naveen Patnaik'* that in 2000 assembly election when he broke the news that Dharmendra Pradhan had won, Naveen said, 'Oh! I've got a problem.' Naveen's prediction regarding Dharmendra Pradhan seems to be coming true after decades.

However, The Congress Party in Odisha has not yet strengthen its organization in Odisha. This time too, The Congress Party does not seem to be in the league, which has been out of power in state for more than 23 years.

But the Bhartiye Janata Party is putting all its strength from state to center for change of power in Odisha, to form government in Odisha. And Dharmendra Pradhan remains its main face from BJP. Mr. Pradhan has emerged as a big challenge for BJD and Naveen.

The election bugle has sounded. A stir has started in the political ocean regarding the 2024 general elections. The water is gradually becoming warm. It is engaged in increasing the political temperature not only in Odisha but in the whole India.

It would not be a mistake to say this, that the amount of heat in Odisha is a little more. Because in Odisha, along with the Parliament elections, Assembly elections are also held. So that's why the Leaders are ready, Public ready and the EVM machine is also ready for the election.

Of course, the election has not been announced yet but the heat of election is seen in the battle field. The post-mortem from getting the party ticket to winning and losing prediction is also starting slowly.

Who will win…?

Who will lose…?

Who will get the ticket…?

The general elections of 2024 are only a few months away, but challenges for major political parties like Biju Janata Dal, Bharatiya Janata party and the Congress are many. Specially for the Biju Janata Dal. It would be a tough test these major three parties to deal with the challenges in the shortest time. Especially this will be a litmus test for the ruling BJD, seems to have more challenges than the opposition this time while the opposition parties need to set right the organizational issues before going ahead with electioneering in the state.

But for the ruling BJD's challenge lists is quit longer than as before. The list of challenge for the BJD is that, it has to tackle multiple ticket aspirants, alleged anti-incumbency wave, infighting, tainted leaders, alleged sway of bureaucracy, a dented image of Chief Minister Naveen Patnaik due to the arrest of several BJD leaders by CBI in the chit fund scam and the other side increasing popularity of Prime Minister Narendra Modi is a big challenge for BJD, Indeed.

If we talk about the general election, then as far as Lok Sabha elections are concerned, the picture is clearly visible. That Prime Minister Narendra Modi has not decreased in any way in his popularity till now. Various surveys have shown that he is still maintaining his popularity. And the report coming from the public shows that his popularity graph has not diminished.

Along with that "Modi Guarantee", recently we saw that elections were held in five states. And there BJP contested the elections by not presenting any specific Chief Minister candidate and contested in the name of Modi. And achieved splendid victory in three major states of

Hindi belt. Rajasthan, Madhya Pradesh and Chhattisgarh, BJP achieve massive success here. This shows that BJP is in a very good position. And the kind of work and publicity going on for Ram Mandir. This shows that along with all other contexts, along with the other welfare schemes, including people's religious sentiments, how can it be converted into vote bank? For this they have made a detailed plan and work is going on accordingly.

For the Bharatiye Janata Party, these three things are in their core context. And this is not today, but from the day of formation of BJP till today, these three are in their main context. In that, removing article-370, which they have already done and the second most important one which had not happened yet and that is 'Construction of Ram Mandir'.

The moment the Supreme Court gave the green signal, and after that the work of temple construction progressed to a great extent and if we can see that with a strong intention to inaugurate the temple at a particular time. "Prana Pratistha" performed on January 22 and the elections are to be held in April and May. And in these two-three months, BJP will try its best to conduct intensive campaign. There is no scope for doubt or dilemma that how much BJP will succeed in its objective. The opposition in center being weak and not organized is one of the major strength of the Bharatiya Janata Party. So picture is almost clear in the center.

But it is true that the situation of state politics in Odisha is still not clear at all. It would be very difficult and hesitating to say at all whether BJP will be able to show its 'Modi Magic' in Odisha or not, but it is not even Impossible!

Yes, there is one thing very clearly visible that BJP had won the number of votes in the last election in Odisha, this time BJP will try to achieve more vote shares in this 2024 election and will successful in it too! So, 2024 elections will not be even so easy for BJD.

We discussed the reason for this above widely but we will end this chapter as well as the book here with one last healthy discussion.

It is very, very clear bright that the NDA will Come Back to power in the center again.

In the state, BJP or Congress have not yet been able to compete or stand parallel with BJD. Congress has not yet been able to organize its organization and BJP still running by confidence and determination.

So, that's why the situation of BJD is strong and ahead in Odisha, no doubt. It can be said with certainty that, because of the way Naveen Patnaik himself had directly operated in the last elections, can't do it right now, due to increasing age. One another thing is that maybe Mr. Pandian's sudden appearance will definitely affect the election result to some extent. Because of course his central role in BJD has created a movement in the minds of some people. Some people inside and outside the party are unhappy with this decision. However, there is no doubt about Mr. Pandian's understanding, ability to work, developing mindset and many more. He already proved himself that how talented he is and how much he is concern about Odisha's development in all aspects but it's just a matter of few people's narrow mindset that he is from another state.

Well, only time will tell to what extent Mr. Pandian's Non-Odia picture will put impact on anything. Because I am a resident of Odisha, I am an Odiya, so it does not matter to me that he is not an Odiya. What matters for me is my state's development, only development from all corners. So I am sure people in Odisha also risen above this conservative mindset.

And the second thing is that even if some people have any complaint about this, even if there is an objection, it should not be an objection to others. Because everyone has the right to express their views and this is the beauty of democracy.

In today's day the biggest challenging issue for BJD is that, for the 147 seats of the Odisha Assembly BJD has more than 1000 aspiring candidate currently. What has been revealed from the initial survey. So, how will such a large number of candidates be managed? In this situation BJD has become burden for BJD itself. How Mr. Pandian will successfully manage this challenge, it is very interesting and important?

So that is why BJD's assessment of 123 plus in coming 2024 elections that is not at all easy and in what quantity it will be right or wrong to say this, time will determine.

And of course the '*Janata*' public will decide!

This is the beauty of democracy that, where the public is all in all, the public is the sovereign and public's decision is above all accepted in democracy. Democracy is a rule where power lies in the hand of the people.

Father of the nation Mahatma Gandhi said, *"I understand Democracy as something that gives the weak the same chance as strong".*

Odisha has been Governed by the same Chief Minister more than 23 years. The second longest serving CM in India, Mr. Naveen Patnaik is now @ 77 plus. He is at second position leaving behind Jyoti Basu of West Bengal. Naveen Patnaik is still only the second. Yet to achieve the milestone.

Maybe this year he will become the longest serving Chief Minister of India by crossing Pawan Kumar Chamling of Sikkim. And then Naveen Babu will reach in the incredible destination, which is highly impossible for any politician in this cut throat era of politics. I hope and wish from the core of my heart that Naveen Babu will cross the milestone soon and definitely he will become the longest serving Chief Minister of India.

Mr. Naveen Patnaik built his party into such a humongous power that nobody has been able to shake him for five elections and this year he will be seeking for his sixth term. The whole Odisha's focus is on whether Mr. Naveen Patnaik will be able to take oath as the Chief Minister of Odisha for sixth time or not.

Although Mr. Patnaik's achievements have been truly remarkable. But still it is very interesting for everyone, because if he wins 2024, he will scale further heights and a far bigger political phenomenon.

Even if he loses this 2024 election, he will still remain a phenomenon.

He had some health challenges in the past. But his mind is all there, he is very sharp, he is very smart, he is fully in control.

May God bless Mr. Naveen Patnaik long life with good health.

Along with the wish and prayers I am going to end this unauthorized biography of our beloved Chief Minister Mr. Naveen Patnaik.

I hope that my years of research and hard work, which is now in your hands in the form of a beautiful book, will be liked by not only Naveen Patnaik's fans and admirers but also his political rivals and opponents.

As per my habit, I would love to write few lines to convey my love and respect for our beloved and respected Chief Minister Mr. Naveen Patnaik.

"Ek Naveen Ne Badle Hain Khwaab, Jo Utkal ke Na Janey Kitney
Khuli Deed Se Dekha Hai, Har Wo Anmol Manjar Na Jane Kitney

Faqr O Naaz Karti Hai Aaj, Baar Baar Apni Har Haashil Pe Odisha
Ki Haqeeqat Main Badley Hain, Kayee Guldastey Sapno Ke Na Jane Kitney

Sirf Ek Khokla Jumla Nahi, Wada Hai Har Ek Wada Tumhara Naveen
Mil Gayi Kayi Khusian, Likhe Gaye Ebarat Sunherey Na-jaaney Kitney

Meetani Jo Chahi Ek Jarra Utkal ka, Kabhi Fani, Hud-Hud Aur Kabhi Failin Ney
Rushwa Loute Sab, Naveen Jo Ban Chuka Tha Odisha Dunya ke Liye Kitney

Koun Koun Se Hain Mansubey Naveen Ke, Kitney, Ek Do Ho To Bataoun Tumhe
Mamta, Kalia, Khusi Se Lekar Harischandra Tak, An'geenat Hain Mansubey Kitney

Gareebi, Bhukhmari, Pichda Jaise Sabd Kabhi Dukhatey They Dil Ko Be-Intehaan
Droupadi, Role Model, Sports Capital Jaise Gulab Ab Shaan Badhatey Hain Utkal Ki Kitney

Aur Log Kehtey Hain, Tum Shaan Ho, Tum Jaan Ho, Tum Swabhimaan Ho Odisha ki
Koi Kuch Bhi Kahey, Tum Sehar Ho Us Tareeki Ki, Dard They Jismain Na Jaaney Kitney"

– **Razique Hosain Shaikh**

Acknowledgement

Bismillah Hir Rehmaan Nir Raheem...

First and foremost, I would like to thank my parents Asira Khatun and Shaikh Gollam Rabani, who educated me, supported me, up brought me with so much love and affection and made me worthwhile to write a book, "Alhumdulillah".

As always I would like to thank everyone who played an important role in my life. Thanks for their endless support, my brothers --- pillar of support in my life, thanks for making me so comfortable that I could think of writing a book.

Shaikh Reyajat Hussain Azhari, CEO Jamia Al Habib, Rasulpur

Shaikh Gayas Uddin, Farmer

Shaikh Saddam Hossain, Project Manager TCS

Shaikh Raish Uddin, Managing Partner, Cater Tech, Dubai

Shaikh Abid Hossain, Chief Accountant, Javaheri Group, Dubai

Shaikh Akmal Hussain, Dealer Indian Oil, Raza Filling Station, Koraput

A word of gratitude also goes to my elder sisters, Imrana Khatun and Sultana Khatun.

A special thanks to; Imam Uddin Shaikh, Managing Director, Cater Tech, Dubai for his tremendous support and motivation.

I would like to express my sincere gratitude to my editor, Mrs. Sohana Saheen Hussain who's a post graduate in commerce and is really great at public speaking, writing and editing. Her expertise and attention to detail truly transformed my work into a polished and refined piece. Her insightful feedback and suggestions were invaluable in helping me to clarify and strengthen the massage of my writing. Her dedication to ensure that my writing is precise and grammatically correct is greatly appreciated. Her passion for her work is inspiration to me, and I look forward to the possibility of future collaborations.

A big thanks to Shaikh Istaque Alli and Shaikh Safaqat Alli for their extraordinary motivation towards writing.

I would like to thank all my readers and well-wishers who supported me and motivated me with their love and kind words.

A very big thanks to the team of Notion Press for believing in my manuscript and converting it into such a beautiful book.

Last but not the least, I would like to thank my wife Falak Ara Begum and my children Zulekha Sadia, Zainab Sadia and Zeenat Sadia for their splendid support and immense patience while I sat late night to write this book.

Thank you all…!

Precious Memories

The Collections of few precious photos and some golden glimpses that summarize how the Naveen era has changed the transformed Odisha.

Courtesy: Newsroom Odisha Network

Young Naveen Patnaik with mother Gyan Patnaik and his legendary father, former CM of
Odisha Mr. Biju Patnaik

Courtesy: Newsroom Odisha Network

A childhood: Prem Patnaik, Gita Mehta & Naveen (from left)

Courtesy: Newsroom Odisha Network

Naveen with former PM Lal Bahadur Shastri, former Odisha CM Nandini Satpathy, sister Gita Mehta and Ajit Mahapatra.

Courtesy: Newsroom Odisha Network

Naveen with Tavleen Singh and Vasundhara Raje

Courtesy: Newsroom Odisha Network

Naveen Patnaik sworn in as Chief Minister of Odisha in 2000

Courtesy: Newsroom Odisha Network

Naveen begins his second term as CM of Odisha

Courtesy: Newsroom Odisha Network

Naveen once again victorious and serves as CM for third time

Courtesy: Newsroom Odisha Network

Naveen takes oath as Odisha's Chief Minister for fourth consecutive time

Courtesy: Newsroom Odisha Network

Naveen invincible: Sworn in as the Chief Minister of Odisha for the record fifth consecutive time

Courtesy: Newsroom Odisha Network

CM Naveen Patnaik at painting function in Bhubaneswar

Courtesy: Newsroom Odisha Network

Inauguration of exhibition Hockey match between Odisha XI vs NSW (Australia) at Biju Patnaik Hockey Stadium

Courtesy: Newsroom Odisha Network

At the IFTAR Party at Bhubaneswar in 2013

Courtesy: Newsroom Odisha Network

CM celebrating Independence Day with school children at Naveen Newas

Courtesy: Newsroom Odisha Network

Naveen Plants Peepal tree in the premises of Lok Seva Bhawan and
coins it 'Freedom Tree' on the occasion of 153rd birth anniversary
of Father of the Nation Mahatma Gandhi

Courtesy: Newsroom Odisha Network

Odisha Chief Minister Naveen Patnaik poses for a group photograph with the Indian hockey team players at a press conference in New Delhi.

Courtesy: Newsroom Odisha Network

Naveen Patnaik felicitates Indian hockey teams Mens and Womens with cash prize after their arrival from Tokyo Olympics, in Bhubaneswar

Courtesy: Newsroom Odisha Network

Odisha CM meets President-elect Draupadi
Murmu in Delhi

Courtesy: Odishatv.in

*Naveen with PM Narendra Modi at the Eleventh meeting of the
Inter-State Council at New Delhi*

Courtesy: Newsroom Odisha Network

CM Naveen Patnaik with Ratan Tata during MoU signing ceremony
for setting up Tata memorial hospital in Bhubaneswar

Courtesy: Newsroom Odisha Network

Naveen participates in the 'Retreat', an exclusive meeting of the Prime Minister with the Chief Ministers

Courtesy: Newsroom Odisha Network

CM Naveen Patnaik reviews progress of heritage corridor project for Puri Jagannath Temple

Courtesy: Newsroom Odisha Network

Naveen Patnaik with Home minister Amit Shah, West Bengal Chief Minister Mamata banerjee, Bihar Chief Minister Nitish kumar and Union Minister for Petroleum & Natural Gas and Steel Dharmendra Pradhan during their lunch at Naveen Niwas

Courtesy: Newsroom Odisha Network

CM Meets with His Excellency Lt. Gen. (Retd.) Andi M. Ghalib,
Ambassador of Republic of Indonesia on 07th Jun 2012

Courtesy: Newsroom Odisha Network

Odisha CM with eminent actor Kamal Haasan in Chennai

Courtesy: Newsroom Odisha Network

Naveen with Reserve Bank of India Governor Shaktikanta Das at Lok Seva Bhawan in Bhubaneswar

Courtesy: Newsroom Odisha Network

CM taking an aerial view of flood situation at Sambalpur

Courtesy: Newsroom Odisha Network

CM inaugurating Dhamra Port

Courtesy: Newsroom Odisha Network

CM Naveen Patnaik receives the certificate of recognition from Guinness Book of World Records for Birsa Munda Hockey Stadium in Rourkela for being the largest fully seated hockey stadium in the world.

Courtesy: Newsroom Odisha Network

The
Great Gulf
Cookbook
An Arabic
Food Lab
Chef Razique Hosain Shaikh

FIRST LOVE LASTS
FOREVER...
An Authentic Rural Love Story
RAZIQUE HOSAIN SHAIKH

Razique Hosain Shaikh
BROKEN   HEARTS
A love story with
a difference...!

Aapana Maney Khusi Ta...?